YEARBOOK 2015
AUTOCAR
THE YEAR'S GREA

A great year of motoring

WE'VE HAD QUITE a 12 months at Autocar. We've driven three of the fastest road cars ever made, witnessed game-changing debuts (an SUV that can handle like a sports car, for instance), said goodbye to some iconic models and welcomed some new stars.

Headlines have been stolen by the trio of hybrid hypercars from Ferrari, McLaren and Porsche, which you can read full verdicts of inside. More than their explosive performance, it's the innovative way in which they scale such heights that makes them so compelling.

And it's innovation that has been a key theme of the industry in 2014; the cars we report on here are all landmarks in one way or another, sometimes more. The super-frugal but rapid BMW i8 sports car, the electric Tesla Model S with Aston Martin-baiting performance, and a gorgeous new lightweight Alfa Romeo called the 4C are among the year's highlights.

Illustrated with stunning pictures over 160 pages, these are the best stories to have

appeared in Autocar magazine, on sale every Wednesday, and on the industry-leading autocar.co.uk website in the past 12 months. We hope you enjoy it.

MARK TISSHAW
Yearbook editor

120
Alfa's new poster boy meets its rivals

116
We say sayonara to Mitsubishi's legendary Evo

CONTENTS

36

Bold and beautiful:
Lamborghini's new V10
supercar put to the test

76 How to turn a family hatch into a racer

96 The only way is up: luxury Pug concept

128 Can the latest 'Vette mix it in Europe?

50 All-new Mini driven for the first time

144 Celebrating 25 years of the Discovery

102

New Mercedes C-class takes on BMW 3-series

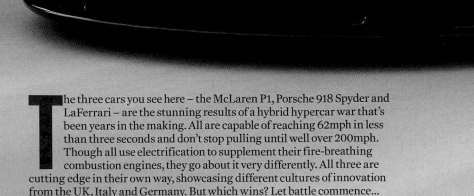

Driven: the world's three fastest cars

The three cars you see here – the McLaren P1, Porsche 918 Spyder and LaFerrari – are the stunning results of a hybrid hypercar war that's been years in the making. All are capable of reaching 62mph in less than three seconds and don't stop pulling until well over 200mph. Though all use electrification to supplement their fire-breathing combustion engines, they go about it very differently. All three are cutting edge in their own way, showcasing different cultures of innovation from the UK, Italy and Germany. But which wins? Let battle commence...

8

14

20

Along came a Spyder

Weissach's 875bhp 918 Spyder is first to reveal its colours in the long-awaited Porsche vs McLaren vs Ferrari hybrid hypercar showdown. **Steve Sutcliffe** gets behind the wheel

In the 918, it takes scarily little effort to keep up with a 911 Turbo S being driven as fast as it will go by Walter Röhrl

Spring 2011 brought us the opportunity to give the then-new Bugatti Veyron Supersport the full Autocar road test treatment. It was a landmark event for numerous reasons, not least of which was that it was the 5000th road test published by this magazine. And at the end of the test we wondered whether any car, at any price, at any point in the future, would ever surpass the Veyron's biblical performance.

And now here we are, about to let rip in the first of three brand-new hypercars, the other two being the McLaren P1 and LaFerrari. Each of these three cars will, it seems, match or beat the mighty Bugatti where it matters most: on the way up to 200mph and around any corner you'd care to aim them at.

Then again, perhaps we shouldn't be so surprised by such an outrageous realisation, given that Porsche claims to have built "the sports car of the future" in the 918 Spyder. Statements such as this don't often come out of Porsche's engineering centre at Weissach unless the results are guaranteed to be spectacular. And believe me, in this case, they are. Oh my goodness, how spectacular they are. Better, indeed, than originally seemed likely.

How so? Because just over a year ago, Porsche announced to the world that the 918 Spyder had lapped the Nürburgring in 7min 14sec, that it could return 94.1mpg on the combined fuel economy cycle and that it developed a walloping 795bhp courtesy of its part-electric, part-petrol V8 hybrid powertrain.

In Hot Laps mode, things happen almost too quickly for the driver to take it all in

Interior follows Porsche's conventions but is befitting of the 918's hypercar status

E-Power mode yields a 0-62mph time of 6.2sec without waking the tachometer

Fast forward to recent weeks, however, and Porsche revised those figures. It said that the final car, while still good for 94.1mpg, would now develop 875bhp and 944lb ft of torque, take three seconds less than it did to reach 186mph and could lap the Nürburgring in a mere 6min 57sec, which is quicker than any other production road car in history. And faster, indeed, than either McLaren or Ferrari has managed to go. Yet.

Make of that what you will, but what matters now is that the 918 Spyder is here, in the metal, in its final specification, costing €781,155 (or around £623,000) in standard specification or €853,155 (around £680,000) in the 40kg lighter 'Weissach Pack' form tested here. And for the time being, it is the fastest road car on the planet.

Porsche's performance claims for the Weissach Pack 918 are nothing short of breathtaking. How about 0-62mph in 2.5sec, 0-124mph in 7.2sec, 0-186mph in 19.9sec and a 215mph top speed? When we road tested the 1183bhp Veyron Supersport in 2011, we recorded equivalent times of 2.6sec (to 60mph), 7.1sec and 18.9sec. According to Porsche's legendary test driver, Walter Röhrl, who was on hand and has vast experience of both cars, the 918 is "quite a lot quicker than the [standard] Veyron up to 180mph", beyond which it's debatable whether anything else matters.

Driving the 918 is a slightly strange experience to begin with, even though one of Porsche's main targets when fine-tuning the car was to make it as natural and intuitive as possible,

despite its complex technologies. In E-Power mode, for instance, you are driven purely by the two electric motors to begin with (one for the front axle, the other for the rear), but this still means you've got enough ecologically sound propulsion to hit 62mph in 6.2sec.

The spooky thing in E-Power, as ever with EVs, is that there's no perceptible noise from the two electric motors. Instead, you just turn the key, select Drive, press the throttle and glide away, looking like the world's most exotic milk float. With the lithium ion battery pack fully charged, you've got about 20 miles of range in E-Power mode.

But if you then press harder on the accelerator – boom! – the V8 is awakened and you find yourself being propelled by a combination of

conventional V8 and electric power. At that point, the monster reveals its true colours and you realise that the 918 is still just a good old-fashioned V8 supercar at its core. The transition is surprisingly smooth, as long as you're not clumsy with the pedal, and if you then back away from the throttle for a few seconds, the V8 will switch off and you're back into 'Hal 9000' mode, listening to the air rushing by and to the massive 265/35 R20 front and 325/30 R21 rear Michelin Pilot Cup 2 tyres rumbling away beneath.

Select Hybrid mode and you get an instant combination of all three power sources, but still with quite relaxed responses from the throttle and the seven-speed dual-clutch automatic gearbox. Choose Sport and the responses from everything – engine, gearbox, V8 and both the electric →

So flat does the 918 Spyder corner, and with so much composure, that it looks undramatic, even when driven at or near its limit. The electric steering is also superbly accurate

← motors – get sharper and keener. Then you can go up again to Race mode and eventually to the Hot Laps program, in which the ESP allows a bit of slip from the rear and dishes out even more torque to the front axle under wide throttle openings to dial out mid-to-late-apex understeer.

But we're getting ahead of ourselves here, because even in less-frisky Hybrid mode, the 918 Spyder still feels at least as quick as any other Porsche currently on sale, if not quicker – at least if you open the throttle wide and hold it there for three or four seconds, allowing the 4.6-litre V8 to rev right out to its deafening 9000rpm limit. But it's the initial hit of torque from the electric motors that provides the shattering responsiveness.

In seventh gear at 50mph, it picks up with the same kind of thump that a GT3 delivers in third at 70mph, no exaggeration. And that's in cuddly old Hybrid mode, remember.

Twist the dial on the steering wheel round to Race and the throttle response goes from 'good' to 'good grief'. And in Hot Laps it goes up a big notch again. At 2500rpm in this maddest mode, the 918 feels uncomfortably explosive in the way it leaps forward at the merest tremble of the throttle pedal, while at 5000rpm it feels twice as energised and three times as potent.

Don't even try to compute what it feels – or sounds – like at 8000rpm in a low gear, because things happen so fast in the first three ratios that you won't actually be able to recall the details. Only by selecting a high gear at low revs is it possible to drink in what occurs in this car in its most potent setting, and even then the din from the V8 is so loud, and the speed with which you are thrust towards the horizon so completely overwhelming, that you might not be able to remember much about that, either. At least not during five laps following a 911 Turbo S that's being driven as fast as it'll go by Walter Röhrl.

What I do remember vividly about driving the 918, though, is how well it disguises its weight. On a track, being driven with sufficient gusto to keep Röhrl in sight (which requires scarily little effort, to be honest, so much quicker is the 918 compared with the 911 Turbo S), it feels like it weighs no more than about 1350kg or 1400kg, rather than the declared 1674kg (in standard form). The way it changes direction is astonishing for something so big. Understeer is pretty much non-existent at sane speeds, and the flatness with which it corners – and the resulting composure – boggles the mind, be that on the way in, on the way through, or on the way out of corners, be they fast or slow.

The steering is also quite brilliant in its accuracy, even though it might lack that last smidgen of feel beside the very best hydraulic systems. Yes, it's electric, and no, it doesn't fizz with feedback through the rim in a manner

reminiscent of a 1990s 911, but this seems vaguely irrelevant in the 918. Things happen so fast in this car that you almost don't have time to bemoan the absence of interaction. The rest of the driving experience is so intense that there really isn't room for a hit of old-school-style feel.

Better still, Porsche would appear to have all but eradicated the artificial brake pedal feel that early prototypes apparently suffered. In production spec, the brakes are much like those of any other Porsche when under duress – fantastic, in other words – even if the pedal does feel a touch remote under lighter loads in EV mode.

In isolation, the 918 Spyder is a really quite fantastic amalgam of ultra-high-tech and conventional engineering and, as a result, provides a hitherto undreamed-of combination of massive performance, reasonable refinement, surprising driveability and quite incredible real-world economy for a car of this kind. But the best bit about it is how natural and pure it feels to drive.

At its core, and despite its dizzying tech, the 918 is just a cracking thing to go out for a blast in. And it's cataclysmically fast, too, without feeling scary, edgy or overwhelming. Most drivers could, after a while, get quite close to what this car can do near its limit. It really is that friendly to drive. The McLaren P1 and LaFerrari will need to be very special cars indeed – freaks, even – to deliver a wider range of abilities than this. **A**

GET WITH THE PROGRAM

"A YEAR AND a half ago we were nowhere with this car," admits 918 project leader Frank Walliser. "To begin with, it took us a long time to understand how all the car's systems could be integrated. But the advance in software quality over the past 18 months has allowed us to get where we have with the car. And today, well, it is what it is. I honestly don't believe it can now be improved."

So the relentless march in the progress of software is the star of the show, and that's from the man who created this extraordinary car. This might seem hard to believe, considering that the 918 has two electric motors, 314kg of lithium ion batteries, a seven-speed dual-clutch gearbox and active aerodynamics. But that's why the software is so vital, because without it, none of these chunks of technology could communicate smoothly.

PORSCHE **918 SPYDER** (WEISSACH PACK)	
VERDICT	★★★★☆
Price	€853,155
	£680,000 (approx)
0-62mph	2.5sec
Top speed	215mph
Power (combined)	875bhp at 8500rpm
Torque (combined)	944lb ft at 4000rpm
Gearbox	7-spd dual-clutch automatic

WORTH THE WAIT

Two decades after it gave us the legendary F1, McLaren is back in the hypercar game at last. **Steve Sutcliffe** finds out just how good the P1 is

The P1 is a quite insanely fast car and, yes, it picks up where the F1 left off

Never will I forget the day on which Autocar first got to drive the mighty McLaren F1. It was 5 May 1994, the day after Ayrton Senna had been killed at the San Marino Grand Prix, and the good people from McLaren – for whom Senna had driven for so long and with such passion – were understandably somewhat subdued to begin with.

But as the day went on and the car began to take centre stage, the atmosphere lifted – because the car itself was beyond incredible. The F1 was the fastest car that any of us had ever sat in, by a very big margin. It blew each and every one of us away.

And now here we are again, 20 years later, out in sunny Bahrain, about to let rip in the all-new McLaren P1, which, if Woking's

claims are to be believed, will rewrite the road car performance rulebook once more. And this time there is nothing but optimism filling the air.

Before I climb aboard the P1, however, I can't help but think back to the end of our three days with the F1. Once we'd finished with it, we at Autocar each wondered if we would ever drive anything quicker than the F1. None of us thought so. We truly believed we'd driven the fastest road car the world would ever see.

Will I feel the same sense of awe at the end of my day with the P1? Maybe, maybe not. But first, let's look at some numbers, most of which will either make you laugh or cry. Or both.

The P1 costs £866,000 and only 375 examples will be built, all of which, claims McLaren, have already found homes. At the P1's core is a

Cabin layout and driving position are like the 12C's, but bespoke controls set it apart

Seats are supportive – and need to be

A limited run of 375 guarantees exclusivity

The P1 drives silently in all-electric mode, but that's a sideshow next to its track skills

two-seat carbonfibre tub, much like that of a Le Mans prototype racing car. It is propelled by two distinctly different power sources. The first is a twin-turbocharged 3.8-litre V8 that produces 727bhp at 7300rpm and 531lb ft at 4000rpm. The second is an electric motor that uses a brace of lithium ion batteries to produce a further 176bhp and 192lb ft. This provides the P1 with combined outputs of 903bhp and 664lb ft.

As you'd expect, the car is made from all sorts of exotic materials beneath its mostly carbonfibre outer skin. The key statistic that results from this is a kerb weight of just 1450kg, which gives it a 623bhp per tonne power-to-weight ratio, and that, says McLaren, is enough to fire the rear-wheel-drive P1 to 62mph in just 2.8sec, 100mph in comfortably

under six seconds and 200mph in less than 20 seconds. Bear in mind that, when we tested the F1 all those years ago, it recorded times of 3.2sec to 60mph, 6.3sec to 100mph and 28.0sec to 200mph and you begin to get some idea about how monstrous the P1's performance really is.

And then there's the actively managed, hydraulically controlled aero package, the vast, retractable rear wing, a super-fast dual-clutch automatic gearbox, carbon-ceramic brakes, phenomenally clever traction and ESP systems and the 'push to pass' and drag reduction systems, none of which were present on the F1 but all of which, McLaren says, make the P1 faster – in some cases a lot faster – than it otherwise would be.

Fast enough to lap the Nürburgring in "considerably less

than seven minutes", says McLaren. Even at this stage of the car's life, Woking still won't say what the car's official Nordschleife lap time is, though 6min 47sec keeps cropping up on the internet rumour mill. But according to a McLaren insider I spoke to who knows rather more about the P1's capabilities than any armchair expert ever could, the actual time is "a fair bit quicker". As in 6min 30-something seconds.

So what's it like to drive, this successor to the F1? And is it a worthy replacement for the original hypercar? On this first brief acquaintance, the answer is pretty clear: the P1 is a quite insanely fast car and, yes, it picks up where the F1 left off, and then some.

I drove it first on the roads in and around Bahrain International Circuit

and then on the grand prix circuit itself (albeit just for a few all-too-brief laps), and I can tell you that the P1 is an unbelievably good hypercar.

On the road, at normal speeds, the first impressions are of a car that feels very like the 12C. Not a bigger, hairier, more evil 12C, but a slightly noisier, slightly stiffer-riding 12C. Fundamentally it feels like the same car. Which is a good thing if you've never driven a 12C or, initially at least, a mild anti-climax if you have.

The driving position and cabin architecture are both instantly familiar. The driver's seat is more supportive than a 12C's, but it clamps you in position in exactly the same way behind a steering wheel that's again different in its detail design but which looks and feels familiar.

The longer you spend behind

obvious the differences become. There are, in fact, lots of bespoke features inside, such as the sea of extra buttons on both the dash and steering wheel that control the car's hybrid system, its IPAS 'push to pass' overtaking feature and Track mode's drag reduction system.

There's also an extra depth of sound from the twin-turbo V8, even when you give it just the gentlest of prods in a high gear. Likewise, the dual-clutch auto 'box feels snappier and more responsive. And best of all, again only to begin with, is what happens when you press the 'E-mode' button. The moment you do, the V8 dies and you're left with the spooky but wonderful realisation that you can drive the P1 in total silence. You can't do that in a 12C.

The P1 only develops 176bhp in pure electric mode, but that's still enough to give it broadly the same level of performance as a warm hatchback. McLaren's testers say E-mode soon becomes the default choice for urban bumbles. The batteries recharge when the

petrol engine engages, the ideal recharge point being on a lightish throttle at just over 4000rpm. Driven thus, the P1 will completely recharge its batteries from empty in approximately two minutes. It takes around two hours to achieve the same result via mains recharging. In reality, you almost never need to plug it in to recharge it.

Ultimately, though, the P1 is not a car to drive slowly. It is about going fast – really, really fast – and this is something it can do with varying degrees of madness depending on

which driving mode you choose. That may sound a little bit digital, but the experience is anything but.

What the various modes allow you to do is build up gradually to what the car is capable of. Were you to stick it in Race mode from the outset and let rip, I'd say 90 per cent of even quite competent drivers would fall off on the first lap. The P1's potential to reach the horizon so much quicker than you think it can really is that great. Initially, therefore, the car is pretty hard to get your head around.

So for the first few laps I set

the chassis to Normal and the powertrain to Track and have the boost system switched on. This gives the best throttle response and the quickest gearshifts but cuts the power back to a mere 727bhp. To summon the full 903bhp, you must press the IPAS button on the steering wheel – but you only do that when the car is pointing perfectly straight.

Out of the pit lane and on to the circuit proper, the P1's ride feels sporting but well damped, stiff yet compliant. The steering is light but super-precise, much like a 12C's, and the brake pedal feels reassuringly firm. Unlike Porsche and Ferrari, McLaren decided not to harvest power to the batteries via regenerative braking because they wanted maximum feel through the pedal, and it shows right away. The P1's brakes – developed in conjunction with McLaren's Formula 1 partner, Akebono – are fantastic.

Through the first few corners, there is no perceptible body roll – just lots of bite from the front end via bespoke Pirelli P Zero Corsa tyres, with a correspondingly faithful

P1 demands commitment and skill from its driver in Race mode, otherwise it will bite

reaction from the tail. Through a tight hairpin there is the merest whiff of understeer (although this is a notoriously dusty circuit) but otherwise the P1 feels glued. You aim it at whatever apex you are hurtling towards, you nail the brakes, it slows down – with more stopping power than you've ever experienced in a road car – then you guide it towards the exit more with your brain than any obvious physical movement from your hands. And that's when the P1 gets interesting. From apex to corner exit and beyond, you become aware of just how much energy there is waiting to be unleashed.

The first time I drive it hard out of a corner, the rear tyres light up and the thing takes me completely by surprise. I actually think I'm about to turn it right around, but the traction control does its business and saves me. After that first hit, that first glimpse into the monster's eyes, I learn to regard the P1 in a very different light. This is not, I rapidly conclude, a Big Daddy version of the 12C. It is a completely different animal. One that will chew you up,

take you for a death roll and then spit you back from whence you just came. And that's in Normal mode.

In Sport and Track modes the chassis responses get that little bit crisper and the steering that little bit more incisive, but the differences are subtle. Race mode, however, is an entirely different prospect. If you think the P1 feels like it's dialled up to 11 in Track mode, Race mode takes it to somewhere on the far side of 20. It feels like a completely different car.

So what is it about Race mode that transforms the P1 so dramatically? For starters, the ride height drops by 50mm. That enormous rear wing deploys so you get a vaguely hilarious 600kg of downforce at 150mph. And on top of all that, the suspension goes up at least two more notches on the stiffness and response scales while the powerplant, if you deselect the boost function, is freed to deliver its full 903bhp and 664lb ft, seemingly at the merest twitch of your right foot. The corresponding leaps in performance, cornering grip and dynamic clarity are, shall we say, impressive. And they were already

pretty mind-bending before you hit the button marked Race.

In this lowered mode – which is technically illegal to use on the public highway because of what happens to the lighting and pedestrian impact areas – the P1 will either terrify you or send you to a place of four-wheeled pleasure that you didn't know existed. It is insanely fast in a straight line, and way more urgent in its response to the throttle than the Porsche 918 Spyder.

But it's during braking, in corners and in particular at corner exits where the P1 feels most other-worldly. The grip through fourth-gear corners and above is frankly ridiculous for a road car, and the way it stops from high speeds is enough to make you feel quite unwell if you're not properly prepared for it. And in Race mode it will also allow you huge doses of opposite-lock wheelspin before the stability or traction control systems intervene. As a result, you feel a lot more alone on the track in the P1 than you do in the 918 Spyder.

In the Porsche, there is an underlying sense that something,

somewhere will eventually take care of you. But in the P1 it's not like that. It feels like it's just you, a steering wheel and a very powerful engine doing whatever it can to unstick the rear tyres – and it's only you, your imagination and your right foot that's separating you from the edge. As a consequence, the P1 feels a fair bit more exciting to drive.

Does that also make it feel less technologically advanced than the Porsche? No. The P1 is a deeply complex car that has all sorts of incredible technology of its own bubbling away beneath its carbonfibre surface. The difference is that the McLaren requires a very big contribution from you, the driver, to give its best, whereas that's not always so in the 918 (which remains a phenomenally impressive car in its own right, by the way).

In other words, you need to be right on top of your game to get the best out of the new McLaren P1, otherwise it will have you for lunch. But if you are, the rewards are utterly unparalleled for the time being.

It's over to you, Ferrari.

McLaren P1	
VERDICT	★★★★★
Price	£866,000
0-62mph	2.8sec
Top speed	217mph (limited)
Power (combined)	903bhp at 7300rpm
Torque (combined)	664lb ft at 4000rpm
Gearbox	7-spd dual-clutch automatic

Ooh la La

The Enzo's successor is finally here. LaFerrari costs over £1 million and has a 950bhp hybrid V12. So just how good is it? **Steve Sutcliffe** straps in to see

PHOTOGRAPHY STUART PRICE

Quite often in life, anticipation of an event can far outweigh the enjoyment experienced when said event occurs. And the prospect of driving LaFerrari at Fiorano has provided me with a unique sense of anticipation during the past few weeks, to a point where I've thought about little else leading up to this moment. Yet in this instance, I'm fairly certain that the event itself – the driving of LaFerrari – is going to exceed my expectations.

And if it doesn't – if, for some peculiar reason, the £1.15 million, 950bhp LaFerrari proves to be somehow disappointing to drive – then my world will be inextricably turned upside down. Because let's face it: if this thing can't do it for you as a car nut, nothing ever will.

Before we travel so much as an inch further, however, some history about LaFerrari. And some facts about it, because, like me, you are going to have to wait just a little while longer before climbing aboard this incredible car.

Designed in-house and engineered almost entirely by Maranello's own fair hand, LaFerrari is, as its name suggests, the ultimate Ferrari. Just 499 will be made during the next two years.

At the centre of the car, behind its two fixed carbonfibre seats, sits a 6262cc normally aspirated V12 engine that generates 790bhp at 9000rpm and 516lb ft of torque at 6750rpm. On their own, these outputs would make LaFerrari more potent than the Scuderia's last V12 F1 car, the 412T from 1995. But also behind and beneath the seats sits a 60kg lithium ion battery pack that, via a 25.7kg electric motor, provides 160bhp and 199lb ft to give a combined 950bhp and 715lb ft.

But entirely unlike its rivals from Porsche (the 918 Spyder) and McLaren (P1), LaFerrari's power unit has been designed to produce its maximum outputs *all of the time*. There is no e-mode that can be engaged as such. Instead, the combustion engine and the Hy-KERS system have been engineered to work as one, with energy being continuously harvested on the move (via the brakes, the ABS system, the traction control system and even the E-Diff) →

Awesome-sounding 6.3-litre V12 and Hy-KERS electric combo generate 950bhp and 715lb ft, so there's astonishing thrust at all revs, but LaFerrari is as easy to drive as a 458

← to deliver full beans, as in 950bhp, whenever you want it.

The prodigious energy is sent to the rear wheels, and the rear wheels only, via a seven-speed dual-clutch automatic gearbox, made for Ferrari by Getrag. This also has an electric motor attached to it, with a dedicated gearset that transmits drive directly to the final drive, reducing the need for a typically vast clutch. The meticulous removal of weight is a key theme, and this is but one example.

As with the P1 and 918, LaFerrari features a carbonfibre tub on to which the engine and suspension are mounted. At each corner, there are double wishbones (carbonfibre at the front) and coil springs with electronically controlled dampers, plus enormous carbon-ceramic disc brakes made by Brembo, 398mm at the front, 380mm at the rear.

Electronics play a huge role in the car's engineering and in the delivery of its vast dynamic repertoire. Wings at the front and rear are actively deployed on the move to provide two radically different running configurations: high and low-downforce modes. Mostly, these exist to provide the maximum amount of grip *and* reduced drag required at any given moment – with a maximum of 360kg being produced at 124mph when cornering, or a minimum of 90kg at 124mph when travelling in a dead straight line. On the move, the car decides how much downforce it needs, not you. But the actively managed wings also play a key role in cooling the engine, batteries, gearbox and carbon-ceramic brakes.

The cabin is a deeply exotic place. It's also more intimate than you might expect. That's because the driving position is so low slung, with a fixed seat but movable pedals and steering wheel. Ferrari claims that the driving position is halfway between that of a normal sports car and an F1 car, with the driver's backside sitting at broadly the same height as his or her toes. It certainly feels very 'single-seater', and the rest of the cabin is in the same vein.

Three different instrument styles can be dialled up within the TFT digital dashboard display, all with the revcounter dominating to varying degrees. Anyone who has ever sat in a 458 will recognise certain elements,

Driving position feels very single-seater

Grip is huge, aided by big downforce in corners, and there's old-school steering feel

but there's a sense of purity inside LaFerrari that elevates it above any of Maranello's other cars. It feels quite a lot like you're sitting inside a very well appointed Le Mans car, with swathes of Alcantara and buttons for the sat-nav where normally you might expect to find switches marked 'rain' or 'pitlane speed limiter'.

But most of all it feels natural. It is both comfortable and intimate at the same time – the perfect environment in which to 'do' driving. It features an almost square steering wheel that is festooned with functions and feels exquisite to the touch – not too thick, not too thin, again covered in soft Alcantara and adjustable, like the pedals, over a vast range of movement. If you can't find a perfect driving position in LaFerrari, you probably shouldn't be driving at all.

Even so, you'll also feel a touch nervous before you twist the key and thumb the starter button for the very first time. I'm proof of that, the prospect even causing my hands to shake ever so slightly.

But that's what a car like this can do to you, before you've travelled so much as a centimetre in it. And ultimately, I guess, that's what cars like this are all about. They are fantasy made real – devices so extreme that they enable very lucky people to live the dream in Technicolor, to stand on the precipice of life on four wheels and take a good look over the edge.

First, though, I'm taken for a manic passenger ride by Ferrari's amiable but quietly unhinged chief test driver, Raffa Simone. In many ways, LaFerrari is his car. It is his feedback right from the beginning and throughout the programme that has helped to make LaFerrari what it

is, so it's only fair that he gets to show me what it can do first.

I'm a shockingly nervous passenger at the best of times, and Simone knows this only too well, so he takes it easy to begin with. Even so, many things become instantly obvious as we drive noisily out of the pitbox at Fiorano and on to the circuit.

One: the damping appears to be quite phenomenally soothing, even though Simone has the manettino dial set to Race. Two: the noise from the V12 is even more magnificent than I'd expected. Three: the seats are beautifully dialled in to the rhythm of the chassis and suspension. Four: the result of this is that you feel as though you glide across the ground, even when he runs one of the Pirelli P Zero Corsa tyres across an inside kerb momentarily. And five: holy smoke, does it feel brisk when – on the out lap, remember – he gives it just the smallest of squirts along the back straight towards the main hairpin.

But that's nothing compared to what happens when he hits the brakes for the hairpin itself. I just hang there momentarily, braced against the seatbelts, teeth clenched, jaw metaphorically on the floor. A fairly predictable expletive then makes its way out of my mouth – and at that point Simone looks across at me and smiles and then tells me that it will be okay. "Trust me," he says. "Trust the car!"

What happens next is frankly ridiculous. And not entirely without drama. We do two laps balls to the wall, during which it becomes painfully obvious that LaFerrari is (a) cataclysmically fast in a straight line, (b) stops even better than it goes, (c) sounds, if anything, even →

The noise from the V12 is even more magnificent than I'd expected

←better than it goes *or* stops and (d) generates rather a lot of grip.

But I've come here to drive, not to be terrified in, LaFerrari, for heaven's sake. So after some slowing-down laps and a fair bit of chat about the car itself from Simone – about how they spent two years making the performance "as easy to access as we could" and about why Ferrari resisted the temptation to fit buttons for 'push to pass' or drag reduction systems, and why they decided to keep the ride height of the car constant at all speeds and in all settings, unlike their arch rivals at McLaren – we climb out and it's my turn.

I'm still vibrating inside slightly from the passenger ride as I prod the starter button, squeeze the huge right-hand gearshift paddle to select first and rumble out on to the track in Race mode. The ride still feels spookily smooth, the steering surprisingly light but bursting with a delicious, old-school kind of feel. The brake pedal also feels light underfoot but is again rippling with feel. And the throttle response the first time I go anywhere near the loud pedal just seems outrageously explosive.

And that's what you get when you integrate electric power with a thumping great V12. At low revs the electricity provides the torque, and provides it instantly, and from there on up – at about 3000rpm – the V12 takes over. Yet the transformation is so smooth that you're unaware of it taking place. Instead, it feels like the car has a 10-litre V12 that somehow has massive low-rev response.

And to begin with, at least, it's the immediacy of its throttle response that pretty much defines what LaFerrari feels like on the move. The torque appears to arrive from the moment you think about opening the accelerator, not when you physically press the pedal, and it requires some getting used to. But once you do – and, to be fair, this happens far faster than you'd think – there is a proper box of secrets to be unlocked.

The sheer thrust that the thing can generate will scare most people to begin with, for example, because it really is monumentally rapid. And it just never lets up. The acceleration and the noise and the violence all just keep on coming at you stronger and louder with every extra revolution of the crankshaft until the limiter intrudes at an ear-splitting 9250rpm. The first time that I run it right up to the limiter in third gear, the hairs on the back of my neck sit bolt upright and it's all I can do not to start screaming uncontrollably.

And yet, in their way, the gearchange, the brakes, the steering, the turn-in, the handling balance and the ride are all every bit as incredible as the engine – sorry, the power unit – and the acceleration that it can produce. You look at what this car has on paper and assume that it is going to be a deeply complicated car to drive, but that's not the case at all.

In many ways, LaFerrari feels as

LaFerrari	
VERDICT	★★★★★
Price	€1.2 million (£1.15 million)
0-62mph	Sub-3.0sec
Top speed	"Above 217mph"
Power (combined)	950bhp at 9000rpm
Torque (combined)	715lb ft at 6750rpm
Gearbox	7-spd dual-clutch automatic

natural and easy to drive as a 458 Italia. Its responses may be massive, its grip vast and its performance envelope borderline insane, but it also feels surprisingly normal in the way that it drives. The electronics are there, but they operate very much in the background. They don't define how it feels or how it drives.

And as for the way that you can learn to play with the car, assuming you are bold enough to rotate the manettino switch all the way around to switch everything off, well, it's just breathtaking. Never before have I driven a mid-engined car that feels so well balanced, so comfortable, when its rear tyres are lit and you've got half an armful of corrective lock applied. In my head, in my world, you

shouldn't be able to drive a car like this like that, but anyone who knows broadly what they are doing behind the wheel could do exactly the same thing in it eventually. And that's because the car has been engineered to allow most people to drive it really hard without scaring themselves.

Thus, the grip that it develops may be huge, but you can feel it come and go to the nearest millimetre. Same goes for the steering, which is hyper-alert but not in the least bit neurotic in its response. Even the performance, although savage, can be accessed predictably. There are no spikes on which to impale yourself, even if the scenery does appear in the windscreen at a quite unbelievable lick, if and when you press the

accelerator hard and hold it there for more than a couple of seconds.

On the road, where I also drive it briefly, LaFerrari feels, if anything, even faster still – to the point where you really do need to choose your moment before squeezing the throttle with anything approaching enthusiasm. But even so, the ride quality is still quite amazingly good, the steering perfectly manageable, the visibility nowhere near as poor as I'd expected it to be, the car's general driveability/usability not much less than that of a 458 Italia. Which is extraordinary, given how much deeper LaFerrari's well runs in all other respects, including the ability to turn heads, which it does more than any car I've ever driven.

Big questions, then: is it better, worse or just different from the P1 and 918 Spyder, and is it a worthy successor to the mighty Enzo?

It's more than a worthy successor to the Enzo. Indeed, it makes the old-timer feel gruesomely under-achieving in most respects and is also a much easier, far sweeter car to drive in the process.

Does that make it a better hypercar than the P1? That's a question we aim to answer properly in the months to come, but my hunch, here and now, is that it will be one heck of a dust-up. Between at least two of the world's most exciting cars.

And in the meantime, be in no doubt: LaFerrari is a true masterpiece from Maranello. Ⓐ

ASTON MARTIN V12 VANTAGE S vs JAGUAR XKR-S GT
Stuart Price

THE YEAR'S BEST IMAGES

Our expert snappers go to extremes to capture stunning pictures every week. Here's our pick of their most beautiful and emotive shots from the past 12 months

MERCEDES CONCEPT S-CLASS COUPÉ
Stan Papior

LAMBORGHINI HURACÁN
Stuart Price

EAGLE E-TYPE LOW DRAG COUPÉ
Stuart Price

CATERHAM SEVEN 620R
Stan Papior

PORSCHE 911 GT3
Stuart Price

**LAMBORGHINI AVENTADOR
ROADSTER VS COUPÉ**
Stuart Price

ASTON MARTIN V12 VANTAGE S
Stuart Price

Rated: the top new cars of 2014

THE McLAREN P1, LaFerrari and the Porsche 918 Spyder weren't the only cars in the class of 2014 that challenged conventions and, indeed, defied what we thought was possible in the motoring universe. We were also served up hot hatches that could outrun supercars, an SUV from Porsche that handled like one of its sports cars, a BMW with both the pace of an M3 and the economy to shame any supermini and a Lamborghini as capable around the circuit as on a trip to the shops. Read about them all – and plenty more to boot – over the next few pages.

70

60

36

72

Lamborghini Huracán

1.5.14, Ronda, Spain **Gallardo replacement takes the fight to Ferrari, McLaren and Porsche**

FIRST VERDICT

A more accomplished supercar from Lambo – and a rather beautiful one

★★★★

SO GOOD

- Old-fashioned supercar noise from its V10 is still lovely
- Monster performance
- Terrific brakes

NO GOOD

- Safety electronics too intrusive
- Understeers too much on a track

TESTER'S NOTE

Engine bay looks weird with speckled RTN carbonfibre finish; it looks like it's mud-splattered. SS

At 7500rpm in third gear, it accelerates like a passenger jet at that moment just before take-off

IT WOULD BE EASY to feel a tinge of sympathy for Lamborghini and its all-new Huracán, what with the wonderful LaFerrari making its debut and the McLaren P1 rewriting just about every rule of the road testing book. But once the hypercar hyperbole has died down, the Huracán will be the most important car that Sant'Agata will produce for at least the next three years and, as such, will sell in vastly higher numbers than the über-machines from Ferrari and McLaren combined.

The styling of the Huracán (pronounced 'Hor-a-can') has been described as subdued by some but, in the metal, it has a simple elegance to it that is both refreshing and intimidating. It looks quite small in the metal, too, even though it isn't at 4459mm long and 1924mm wide, and as a replacement for the 11-year-old Gallardo – of which some 14,000 were made between 2003 and 2013 – it borrows more than one or two ideas from both the existing Audi R8 and its replacement, which is due in 2015.

The Huracán's chassis, for example, will be shared with the next-generation R8 and uses a hybrid combination of RTN carbonfibre and aluminium (see sidebar), which, claims Lamborghini, provides it with almost as much strength and stiffness as a full carbonfibre tub but with nowhere near the same expense. It's also far easier and cheaper to repair.

The engine is a development of the familiar 5.2-litre V10 that we've come to know and love in both the R8 and the Gallardo, albeit with a raft of modifications to its top end and exhaust system. This time around, it produces a thunderous 602bhp (or 610PS, hence the LP610-4 moniker) and 413lb ft of torque, which is

The cabin is classier than the Gallardo's, and the gearshift paddles are much larger

sufficient to fire the four-wheel-drive Huracán to 62mph in a mere 3.2sec and to a claimed top speed of 202mph. Stop-start also becomes a standard fitment to help reduce emissions and improve economy by over 10 per cent.

The seven-speed dual-clutch automatic gearbox is also lifted straight from the R8 and replaces, at last, the clumsy six-speed automated manual from before. Which means that a traditional manual gearbox isn't even available as an option in Lamborghini's most popular car.

As on the Gallardo, there are double wishbones at each corner, electronic dampers and anti-roll bars at either end. But this time, these are joined by standard-issue carbon-ceramic brake discs and a new 'Anima' button (which means 'soul' in Italian), similar to Ferrari's manettino dial, that sits dead centre on the bottom of the steering wheel and alters the responses of the dampers, engine mapping, steering, gearbox and traction control. The Anima system offers three different modes to choose from: Strada, Sport and Corsa.

The cabin of the Huracán is deeply Lamborghini in both look and feel. It features a pair of ultra-supportive bucket seats and a dramatic but highly effective new 12.3-inch digital TFT screen that can be tailored to whatever mood you might be in. The gearbox paddles are far larger than before but they are still fixed, so they don't move with the wheel à la McLaren 650S. The visibility out is also better than its predecessor in all directions and there is a sophistication inside – a sense of genuinely high quality – that the Gallardo never quite nailed.

Even so, when you thumb the starter button and the V10 engine catches, there is still the same sense of theatre in evidence as there was with the Gallardo. Like it or not, there is an almighty burst of revs at start-up, and even once the V10 has settled to its idle speed of just under 1000rpm, there's still an old-fashioned supercar kind of racket to be heard from behind your head. And the Huracán wouldn't be a Lamborghini were this not so.

On the move, the car instantly feels more refined but also more →

Mixing carbonfibre with aluminium

LAMBORGHINI WOULD HAVE liked to build the Huracán's chassis purely out of RTN carbonfibre, which is cheaper than traditional carbonfibre because it is pressed rather than cured, but is still far lighter and stronger than any metal. But for reasons of cost and practicality – carbonfibre tubs are far harder to repair, for instance – it went for what it calls a 'hybrid chassis'.

The spine of the transmission tunnel and most of the rear bulkhead is made from RTN carbonfibre, while an aluminium spaceframe makes up the rest. Result: a chassis that weighs 10 per cent less than a Gallardo's but is 50 per cent stiffer and costs almost no more to produce. A rather good compromise, then.

It's a more modern, capable car, but still a hairy-chested Lambo at heart

← comfortable than the Gallardo. There's a new level of maturity to the ride, steering response (no kickback whatsoever), throttle weighting and even the exhaust note that elevates it well beyond its predecessor. But beneath the sheen of smoothness and civility, there is still the raging heart of a conventional V10 supercar, thumping away, itching to be let loose.

And with 602bhp with which to propel just 1532kg of car and the benefits of four-wheel drive to maximise traction, the Huracán is properly fast. There are no peaks or troughs to its power delivery. Instead, it just goes harder in each gear with every extra rev that's added.

At 3000rpm in seventh, it pulls exceedingly well and sounds all grumbly-nasty. At 7500rpm in third gear, it accelerates like a passenger jet at that moment just before take-off and sounds not unlike a Formula 1 car of 10 years ago, with an ear-splitting howl out of its exhaust but also a smoothness to the delivery that was entirely absent from the Gallardo.

All the fizzes and vibrations that used to send shockwaves through the chassis and into your chest and head are gone, replaced by a just as loud but far more soothing mechanical personality. And there will be one or two diehards who won't warm to the Huracán as much as they did the Gallardo as a result.

The ride, handling and steering have gone down a similar route, too. The electro-mechanical steering, for example, has a new variable-ratio rack that, via a central ECU, monitors everything that the car is doing and delivers, says Lamborghini, the perfect response to every input. The same thing goes for the new magnetorheological dampers, tuned to provide the best compromise between ride comfort and handling control no matter what the of surface.

This time, though, you get the distinct impression that the car's numerous electronic systems are very much there to help out if things go wrong. Ironically, the car feels so much less edgy and more rounded in its resolve that you probably don't need the digital safety net to be anywhere near as great.

But that's the way Lamborghini knows it needs to play things in 2014. The vast majority of its customers, many of whom live in China, simply aren't interested in scaring themselves every now and again. Instead, they want a car that looks beautiful (tick), sounds amazing (tick), is relatively easy to drive and live with every day (tick) and won't bite their arms off if they make a mistake in it (tick).

The compromise is that the Huracán probably understeers a touch more than a purist would want it to, and its electronics seem set up to intrude at the slightest whiff of a slide, which is why, on the bumpy road we used for our photos, it felt a bit like driving a car that was being controlled by someone else. And that's not what we want from a Lamborghini.

Also, the engine note does sound more Ingolstadt than Sant'Agata on occasions, particularly on overrun in Corsa mode, when you get a digitally perfected crackle that sounds neither natural nor spine-tingling.

But in just about all other respects and, as it turned out, on most other

roads, the Huracán represents a huge leap forwards for Lamborghini. On smoother, faster, more open roads, it feels pretty damned lovely to drive. And very, very quick. With a far better gearbox than of old, delicious levels of feel and power from its new carbon-ceramic brakes and – best of all, perhaps – a nice, natural feel to its complex new steering rack.

And when you play with the three settings within its new Anima system more extensively – Strada is comfortable, Sport is just that, and Corsa gives a much harder ride and sharper responses – you soon realise that the baby Lamborghini's personality is far more accommodating this time around.

Crucially, at £181k, the Huracán is also very competitively priced beside its key rivals from McLaren and Ferrari, even if the new R8 and current Porsche 911 Turbo will and already do make it seem fairly expensive.

What matters most, though, is the way that it drives: for the most part, beautifully. The Huracán may be a more complex machine than its forebear was – aren't they all nowadays? – but it's also a more modern and capable car than the Gallardo. Yet it's also still a proper, hairy-chested Lambo at heart. And that's really rather refreshing.

STEVE SUTCLIFFE

LAMBORGHINI HURACÁN LP610-4	
Price	£180,720
0-62mph	3.2sec
Top speed	202mph
Power	602bhp at 8250rpm
Torque	413lb ft at 6500rpm
Gearbox	7-spd dual-clutch automatic

No, it's not in camo – that's the characteristic dappled finish of RTN carbonfibre

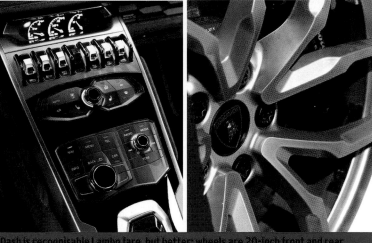

Dash is recognisable Lambo fare, but better; wheels are 20-inch front and rear

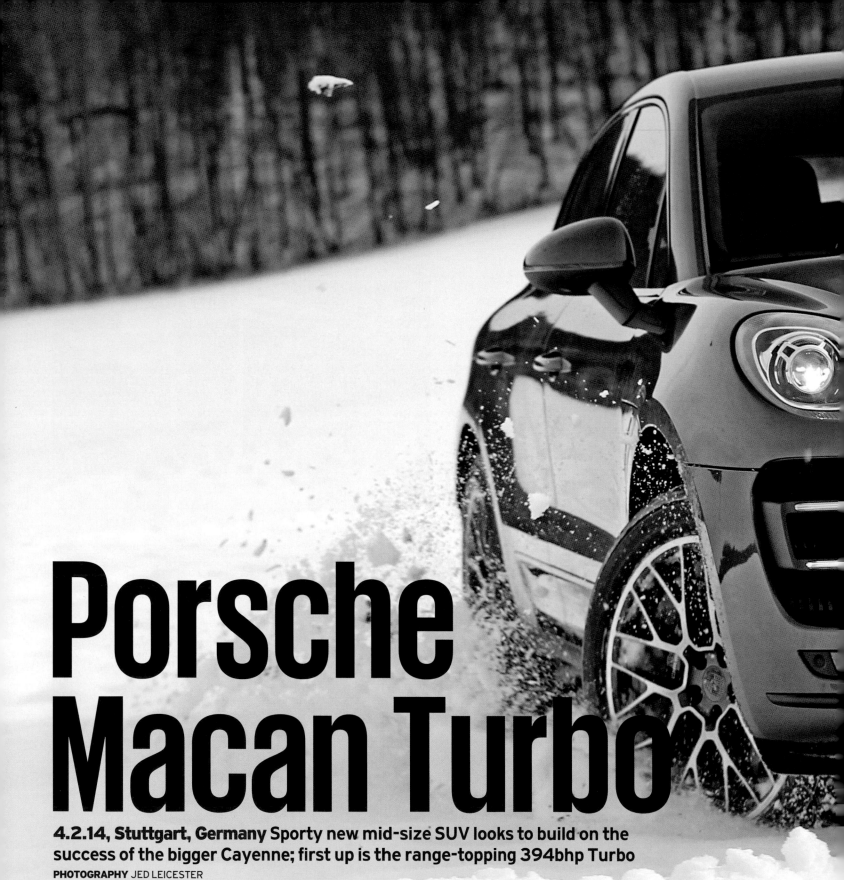

Porsche
Macan Turbo

4.2.14, Stuttgart, Germany Sporty new mid-size SUV looks to build on the success of the bigger Cayenne; first up is the range-topping 394bhp Turbo

PHOTOGRAPHY JED LEICESTER

WHEN THE CAYENNE joined its line-up in 2001, Porsche reaped the rewards of hitherto unrealised demand for an SUV sprinkled with some sports car magic. It went on to become the firm's fastest-selling model ever. Now Porsche is launching the smaller and more affordable Macan. Like its larger sibling, the Macan has been conceived to be more sporting than any existing rival and Porsche hopes that it will carve out an even more lucrative niche for itself than the Cayenne did.

First impressions are of the Macan's relatively moderate size. The dimensions vary slightly between models, but the Turbo tested here is 4699mm long, 1923mm wide and 1624mm high. That makes it 146mm shorter, 17mm narrower and 76mm lower than the second-generation Cayenne. But whereas the Cayenne shares its underpinnings with the Volkswagen Touareg, the Macan is based around a modified version of the high-strength steel platform that underpins the Audi Q5. The two share a 2807mm wheelbase – 88mm shorter than the Cayenne's – but they have little else in common.

The Macan also receives its own mechanical hardware, consisting of specially tuned or unique engines, new gearboxes and a revised version of the Cayenne's multi-plate-clutch

Styling is as 'Porsche' as the response from the turbocharged V6, which is laden with torque and happy to rev but aurally bland

The defining aspect of the Macan Turbo is its handling. If there is a more fluid SUV, I've yet to drive it

four-wheel drive system. The Macan's MacPherson strut front and multi-link rear suspension is also described as unique, with track widths that are up by 35mm at the front and 36mm at the rear over the Q5's.

The new Macan's bold styling takes a number of aesthetic cues from the second-generation Cayenne, including a rather bluff front end that varies in look depending on engine. A large clamshell-style bonnet aids engine bay cooling and features two oval-shaped cut-outs for the headlights plus sides that run all the way down to the front bumpers.

Further back, the plunging roofline creates a coupé-like silhouette that is enhanced by a heavily angled tailgate,

and the rounded rear is dominated by three-dimensional tail-lights that wrap around into the sides. If the muscular design was compromised by the need to share components with the six-year-old Q5, it doesn't show.

Predictably, the interior exudes an upmarket feel. The look again draws heavily on the Cayenne, but subtle changes help set the Macan apart, including a multi-function steering wheel similar to the 918 Spyder's. The rest is familiar, with a three-dial binnacle, touchscreen multimedia system and a high-set middle console housing a sea of switches. It looks cluttered, but the ergonomics are excellent. A low driving position enhances the sporting feel and there's

plenty of adjustment for both the firm front seats and the steering wheel. Visibility is also good, despite the heavily angled rear screen.

The sloping roof doesn't impede rear headroom thanks to a low-set bench, and there's a good deal of legroom. But although the rear seat provides adequate space for the outer two passengers, the middle position is heavily compromised by the centre tunnel. Boot capacity is put at 500 litres – 40 litres less than the Q5 and 170 litres less than the Cayenne.

The early Macan line-up will offer the choice of three V6 engines. Included is a Porsche-developed twin-turbo 3.0-litre petrol unit delivering 335bhp and 339lb ft in the Macan S and an Audi-sourced 3.0-litre turbodiesel with 254bhp and 427lb ft in the Macan Diesel S.

Driven here is the range-topping Macan Turbo. Power comes from a twin-turbo 3.6-litre petrol V6 that is described as being all new, although a non-turbo version of the same unit →

Low driving position instills a sporting feel and there's plenty of seat adjustment; fascia may look cluttered, but the ergonomics are spot on

V6 revs with relish all the way to the 6700rpm limiter

Adaptive damping is standard, air springs are optional

← has appeared in the Panamera. Here, it produces 394bhp at 6000rpm and 405lb ft from 1350rpm.

The engine is pleasingly smooth, potent through the mid-range and accepting of high gears at low speeds. There's some low-end lag, but the new V6 is terrifically energetic on boost. With a short-stroke design, the engine also revs with great conviction for a forced-induction unit, rushing up to 6700rpm without feeling remotely breathless before hitting the limiter.

It is just a pity that the new V6 sounds so characterless no matter which driving mode – Standard, Sport and Sport Plus are offered – is chosen. There is an entertaining burble to the exhaust, but it is more often than not drowned out by excessive induction blare. You wouldn't call it bland, but the noise is rather insipid.

The engine impresses, but it's the standard seven-speed dual-clutch automatic gearbox that really shows its class. It is fast, smooth and intuitive and has the ability to perfectly match revs on downshifts. The Macan's four-wheel drive system directs torque to the rear wheels and, when

the conditions call for it, to the fronts, giving it a distinctly rear-drive bias. Depending on prevailing traction, up to 100 per cent of torque can be sent to either the front or rear wheels. There are also standard traction and stability control systems as well as optional torque vectoring that continuously varies the amount of drive sent to each rear wheel for added traction and increased cornering speeds.

Despite a kerb weight of 1925kg, the Macan Turbo can hit 62mph from rest in a claimed 4.6sec and 100mph in 10.9sec. Porsche doesn't limit the top speed of its production models, and the same is true of this SUV, which is claimed to reach 165mph. Even so, this most powerful of Macans is also relatively economical. Official figures claim 31.7mpg combined. Driven briskly over a mix of urban streets, autobahns and country roads, we returned an indicated 25.8mpg.

The defining aspect of the Macan Turbo, however, is its handling. If there is a more fluid and engaging SUV, I've yet to drive it. Sitting on firm yet forgiving steel-sprung suspension, this SUV delivers an unusually →

← high level of interaction and truly exceptional dynamic qualities.

You can fling the Macan Turbo down a back road at a decent clip and it responds beautifully, offering generous feel and a good deal of feedback through electro-mechanical steering that's wonderfully weighted and engaging. Agility and poise is outstanding for a car of this weight.

It is no surprise that there is some body roll in corners, but the movements are superbly controlled and progressive. The Macan encourages you to keep pushing at the kind of cornering speeds that would leave most rivals trailing.

Our test car ran on optional 20-inch rims with 265/45 tyres up front and 295/40 rubber at the rear, and their outright grip and traction, combined with the rear-biased four-wheel drive system, even on bumpy surfaces, is extraordinary. Deft calibration of the electronic stability control means that the Macan willingly entertains oversteer in Sport mode. Switch into Sport Plus and it becomes even more playful. Meanwhile, away from winding roads, the Macan possesses terrific high-speed stability all the way up to its claimed maximum.

The Macan Turbo's on-road excellence goes a long way towards redefining class standards, and the 'sports utility vehicle' tag was never applied as fittingly as it is here. It is less a junior Cayenne and more a high-riding Cayman in terms of sheer handling proficiency.

The brakes – here, 360mm ventilated discs up front and 356mm ventilated discs at the rear – are no less remarkable. There is a firm but lovely, progressive feel to the pedal, allowing you to confidently tip in the stoppers all the way to the point where the anti-lock begins to cycle.

Not that the Macan Turbo is exclusively sporting. Thanks to the standard fitment of Porsche's variable damper system, PASM, it also offers good everyday comfort. The ride suffers a little around town, but as soon as you hit motorway speeds its pliancy improves. Optional air suspension is claimed to bring a more cosseting ride. We've yet to try it, but experience with the Cayenne suggests that it will be even smoother.

It is unlikely that many Macan buyers will venture far off road, if at all, but a brief run in deep snow revealed that it is quite useful away from the asphalt. An off-road button allows you to alter the threshold of the traction and stability control systems as well as the four-wheel-drive and optional torque vectoring systems.

Porsche claims approach and departure angles of 24.8deg and 23.6deg respectively for the Turbo, while nominal ground clearance is put at 198mm and ramp angle is 17.1deg. Air suspension extends these values.

Despite the odd flaw, it is hard not to get wrapped up in the overall brilliance of the new Macan Turbo. Granted, it is no bargain, but when an SUV is this good, it's easy to believe that it will succeed. If the Macan Diesel and Diesel S are anywhere near as engaging, it won't be long before the Cayenne is supplanted as the fastest-selling Porsche of all time.
GREG KABLE

PORSCHE MACAN TURBO (SPORT CHRONO)	
Price	£59,300
0-62mph	4.6sec
Top speed	165mph
Power	394bhp at 6000rpm
Torque	405lb ft at 1350rpm
Gearbox	7-spd dual-clutch automatic

A low-set bench means rear headroom is good, as is legroom in the two outer seats

Mini Cooper

28.1.14, Puerto Rico **Brilliant three-cylinder petrol engine heads the list of the new Mini's charms**

THIS IS THE moment we've been waiting for, ever since the wraps came off the third incarnation of the modern Mini late in 2013. It is the first time that anyone outside the company has experienced the new three-door hatchback on public roads. Predictably, Mini suggests the new Cooper, the largest and most powerful ever, is well prepared to continue the huge success of predecessor.

Certainly, from the snug confines of the optional sport seats, it is hard to argue that the new Cooper is anything but a huge step forward. From behind its classy multi-function steering wheel – itself part of a significant rethink of the interior – the driving experience is welcomingly familiar. But there is also a new-found maturity and sense of quality that make the car even more pleasant to be in and a good deal more rewarding to drive.

The 1.5-litre three-pot turbo petrol unit is one of four all-new three and four-cylinder engines developed by BMW that will find their way into the new Mini. They share a common architecture, with an aluminium block, individual cylinder capacity of 500cc and 91mm bore centre spacing, that allows them all to be assembled on the same line.

The Cooper's engine is a belter, serving up poke and user-friendliness beyond its relatively conservative power output. As fitted here, it produces 134bhp at 4500rpm and 162lb ft at just 1250rpm, which is 15bhp and 44lb ft more than the naturally aspirated 1.6-litre four that it replaces. The launch range also includes a 1.5-litre three-cylinder diesel in the 114bhp Cooper D and a 2.0-litre four-cylinder petrol engine in the 189bhp Cooper S. A four-pot diesel is expected later, while a 101bhp version of the petrol 1.5 and a 94bhp 1.5 diesel will go into entry-level One models shortly after launch.

The new three-pot in the Cooper is a little vocal at start-up, with a deep thrum from the engine and a distant pulsing of the exhaust as you thumb the starter, now among the toggle switches mounted low on the centre console. However, these qualities are quickly replaced by a more satisfying cacophony as you tip in the revs.

It is a terrifically responsive engine, offering lively pull from little more than 1000rpm all the way to its 6400rpm cut-out. There is a fleeting moment of lag just above idle, but the flexibility and vivacity that follows makes the peaky nature of the four-cylinder engine it replaces seem incredibly old fashioned. The new engine is also delightfully entertaining and has a quite extraordinary operating range, giving the Cooper solid acceleration allied to a wonderfully relaxed nature when pulling taller gears.

It is mated to a new six-speed manual gearbox that has a shorter travel and a more positive feel than its predecessor. A further development is the inclusion of automatic rev

The new Cooper rides with far more pliancy than its predecessor; it's also quieter, more refined and easy natured at a fast cruise, but has lost none of its entertainment value

matching for smoother downshifting. There is no sign of a dual-clutch automatic gearbox, but there is a new optional six-speed torque converter auto, which can be mated with a satellite navigation system to determine which gear best suits a section of road via topography and speed limit data.

At 1085kg, the new Cooper is 10kg lighter than the old model, giving an improved power-to-weight ratio. This is reflected in the quicker 0-62mph time, which drops from 9.1sec to 7.9sec with the six-speed manual gearbox, or an even sharper 7.8sec with the auto. Despite the extra performance, combined fuel consumption and CO_2 emissions have improved by 17 per cent at a claimed 62.8mpg and 105g/km.

A further upside to the new engine is a tangible improvement in refinement, providing the Cooper with a quieter and more relaxed nature throughout the rev range. Combined with better aerodynamic and rolling acoustics, this helps to provide it with more endearing long-distance qualities.

Although its appearance might suggest otherwise, the new Mini has been developed from the ground up. It sits on a new high-strength steel platform, called UKL (for 'Unter Klasse'), that will not only have a huge impact on the future line-up but also underpin the first-ever front-drive BMW. Additionally, the Mini receives wider tracks than before (by 42mm at the front and 34mm at the rear), along with a new MacPherson strut front and multi-link rear suspension. The aim is to sharpen up responses while at the same time providing added ride comfort and refinement.

Despite the clear familiarity of the styling, it is quite a striking car when seen out in the open. The upright cabin and squat stance give it the sort of presence not apparent in any other small car. Yet there is a clear step between old and new, despite the common proportions. All of the traditional design elements are present: the hexagonal grille, round headlights, clamshell bonnet, upright windscreen, floating roof and continuous band of chrome at the base of the glasshouse.

The unadorned body sides also survive, but they now feature tauter surfacing. There is also a new sense of precision to the feature lines, added muscularity within the wheel arches, and the head and tail-lights carry new LED graphics. It is all terrifically poised and confident-looking, especially on the optional 17-inch wheels fitted to our test car (15s are standard, but anything up to 18s are available as options).

But the new Mini is not without controversy. The nose is an odd mishmash of shapes, shutlines and horizontal elements, and the rear lights are comically oversized. Due to increasingly severe crash test regulations, it has also grown quite appreciably. At 3821mm long, →

Cabin quality and ergonomics have improved; three-pot punches above its weight

Styling draws on familiar themes, but it looks more tautly defined and eye-catching than the old model; overall, it is 98mm longer and 44mm wider

←727mm in width and 1415mm in height, it is 98mm longer, 44mm wider and 7mm taller than before. The wheelbase is 28mm longer than that of the old Mini, at 2495mm.

The interior retains the same retro styling theme as before, but it has been greatly improved with new materials and expensive new options. Larger doors help to ease entry, although the seats are now mounted slightly lower. There's greater adjustment to the steering wheel and both front seats, too.

Mini makes a big noise about the overall lift in fit and finish, but it is the ergonomic enhancements that make the cabin a success. Little things, such as the relocation of the main instruments from the centre dial to directly in front of the steering wheel, make the new Mini more intuitive to operate, although it continues to lack oddment storage spaces and the seat adjuster is incredibly fiddly. However, there's more interior space now, as well as a larger 211-litre boot, the capacity of which can be extended by placing the rear seat backrests in a so-called 'cargo' position.

For the first time, the Mini comes with the option of electronically controlled damping that offers the choice between Sport, Mid and Green modes. As with the outgoing model, the driver can also sharpen the steering and throttle response via an optional Driver Experience function. Meanwhile, the Mini's ZF-sourced electromechanical steering system has been re-engineered. A standard speed-sensing Servotronic system reduces the level of assistance at higher speeds for better feel, and there's an anti-torque-steer function aimed at dialling out on-throttle steering corruption caused by the significantly more potent new line-up of powertrains.

One of Mini's key aims with this third generation car was to provide it with a broader mix of manoeuvrability, ride comfort and body control while retaining the agility of the old car. We will need more miles in more familiar surroundings before we can definitively say if it has succeeded, but after a day on Puerto Rican roads, it is clear that the Cooper is more delicately balanced, much smoother-riding and even more entertaining to drive.

It retains the engaging nimbleness and liveliness of its predecessor around town, but from the very first mile you are aware of greater pliancy and absorption within the suspension. Best of all, it has lost none of its high-speed handling prowess. In fact, it has been enhanced, with the new suspension providing a distinctly calmer feel and the revised geometry at the rear giving a more secure feel through corners, both under load and on a trailing throttle. Grip levels are very impressive, too, allowing you to carry a good deal of momentum into bends without understeer or troubling the stability control system. And with a lower centre of gravity and new

Mini Cooper S

Hot new Mini packs a bigger engine to good effect

MINI COOPER	
Price	£15,300
0-62mph	7.9sec
Top speed	131mph
Power	134bhp at 4500rpm
Torque	162lb ft at 1250rpm
Gearbox	6-spd manual

hollow anti-roll bars front and rear, the Cooper possesses outstanding body control. The steering, meanwhile, is better than the old car's, imparting lighter yet more communicative feel along with less kickback and a greater eagerness to self-centre.

So can this third-generation Mini rise above its predecessors and, like them, become a true driver's favourite? In Cooper form, the answer is unequivocal. It has upped the stakes in terms of performance and handling but brings with it a broader appeal thanks to its improved ride quality and everyday usability. It is now a more rounded car than ever before as well as a real entertainer, whether tooling around town or out on the open road.
GREG KABLE

FIRST VERDICT

Quick and great fun to drive, but the ride isn't as good as the Cooper's

★★★★☆

THE FASTEST AND most powerful of Mini's initial line-up of third-gen models is the new Cooper S. Every other new Mini in the launch range has three-cylinder power, but the Cooper S uses a four-pot, albeit a more advanced one than its predecessor's.

The 1998cc, direct-injection petrol engine is twin-scroll turbocharged and 400cc bigger than the unit it replaces, making it the highest-capacity petrol engine ever to be offered in the Mini hatchback. It is, however, 7kg lighter.

Power is up by 8bhp to 189bhp, but more apparent is the increase in torque, which rises by 15lb ft to 206lb ft at 1250rpm. Mini claims

Automatic gets wheel-mounted paddles

0-62mph in 6.8sec and a top speed of 146mph, making the new Cooper S a respective 0.2sec and 4mph faster than its predecessor in as-tested six-speed automatic guise.

A series of exterior styling touches mark the Cooper S apart. Included are a deeper front bumper with a larger horizontal duct, the signature bonnet scoop, rally-inspired graphics, wider sills and a set of 16-inch alloy wheels.

Inside, there is a nicely shaped leather-bound tiller, unique dial graphics and more supportive seats.

The sporting nature of the Cooper S is evident the moment you fire up the engine. Although it lacks the flexibility of the Cooper's new three-pot, it does offer improved low-end response, added mid-range pep and a more involving character than before.

The added performance and responsive nature of the contemporary underpinnings make the new Cooper S fun, fast and nimble. But, as with the standard Cooper, it is also more mature, and the steering, now with speed-sensitive assistance as standard, is lighter in feel but accurate and satisfyingly direct.

But what's really evident is the added security that has been engineered in. You can spear headlong into a tightening corner and lift off sharply without being concerned

about the rear end stepping out of line. When it does begin to slide, it does so in a progressive manner, and there is greater clarity in the way the Cooper S behaves at the limit. However, although the ride is smoother than that of the outgoing Cooper S and has a slightly more forgiving feel, it remains quite firm and its damping lacks the subtlety of the new Cooper's.

The danger in developing new cars from scratch is that they can fail to live up to the reputation of their predecessor. That is not the case here. If you cherish driving or are an existing Cooper S owner, the chances are that you're going to love this third-generation model. It has been improved in every key area and is undeniably more fun to drive. Still, if you're seeking simple everyday usability in a no less entertaining car, the born-again Cooper may well fit the bill at a more affordable price.
GREG KABLE

MINI COOPER S AUTOMATIC	
Price	£20,150
0-62mph	6.8sec
Top speed	146mph
Power	189bhp at 4700rpm
Torque	206lb ft at 1250rpm
Gearbox	6-spd automatic

Volkswagen Golf R

22.1.14, Arvidsjaur, Sweden Range-topping Mk7 Golf gets all-wheel drive and 296bhp to take on the current bounty of red-hot mega-hatchbacks

FIRST VERDICT

Golf refinement, a stonking engine and secure but engaging handling

★★★★☆

SO GOOD

- Usable and well mannered
- Great all-weather traction
- Stealthy Q-car styling

NO GOOD

- Handling could be sharper and more communicative
- Not quite as quick as some

TESTER'S NOTE

Stability control is fully switchable; on a GTI, it reactivates under braking even when 'off'. **MS**

YOU HARDLY NEED me to tell you much about the new Volkswagen Golf R. That it'll be fast goes without saying. These are times when even full-house hot hatchbacks that don't dip below the 5.0sec to 62mph marker are practically failures before they've hit the showrooms. Not to be outdone by its opposition, VW has made its latest 296bhp 4x4 mega-Golf hot enough to hit 62mph in just 4.9sec – if you have the dual-clutch automatic version with launch mode.

You can probably guess, too, that this car will be well built, well equipped, comfortable and easy to use. Despite only having driven it on a frozen lake in northern Sweden, I am as sure of all those things as I am of having driven the car at all.

But is it exciting? Can it immerse you in a point-to-point blast as completely as a Renault Mégane 265 Cup, a Mercedes-Benz A45 AMG or even a Ford Focus ST? The previous Golf R didn't. The current Golf GTI doesn't. And such things come about

as naturally to more ordinary versions of Wolfsburg's European sales champion as a witty one-liner does to a crestfallen cabinet minister.

Besides increasing power output from the Golf GTI's EA888 engine by a hefty margin, VW's R Performance arm has taken 5mm out of the GTI's ride height for the R. It has also reappraised the specification and tuning of both the standard passive and optional adaptive suspension systems, developed a Race mode for the drive select system for even sharper responses and fitted a new electro-hydraulic all-wheel-drive system with 'XDS+' brake-actuated torque vectoring (see sidebar, right).

However, confirming what such promising ingredients amount to will have to wait. Ice driving provides impressions of limited relevance to UK buyers, especially when supplied by a test car on smaller-than-standard wheels and studded snow tyres. It's huge fun, but you don't learn much.

What was unmistakable on first

A frozen lake and studded tyres masked the Golf R's true abilities, but it remained impressively controllable and entertaining

Cabin is superbly executed in the VW style

Golf GTI's EA888 engine gains a full 79bhp

acquaintance was the traction, thrust and red-blooded growl of a mighty powertrain, the muscular civility of a chassis that could be enjoyed in comfort on a daily basis and some remarkably secure on-limit handling manners that cleverly mix directional stability with throttle adjustability.

The new Golf R is quick, then, but on the few occasions when there was enough traction to feel it pulling hard, it didn't seem quite as savage as the A45 AMG does, or as the Audi RS3 did. However, the engine bears comparison with any turbo four in response and high-revving flexibility, and it's got a talent for the dramatic way beyond that of the GTI.

On compacted snow and ice, the car's body control was entirely untroubled by the limited lateral loads it was possible to produce. Its steering was weighty and precise, if a bit muted. The chassis seemed slightly short on bite when first turning in but was governed by an excellent stability system ideally tuned for low-grip conditions in ESC-Sport mode.

The driveline, meanwhile, makes lurid limit handling singularly straightforward, should owners ever be in a position to indulge in it. Keep some positive steering angle dialled in through a corner and the R will glide into a long drift, slipping to angles you wouldn't expect while remaining gently steerable on the throttle. Straighten the wheel and sideways momentum fluently turns into traction and forward speed. Your attitude control isn't as delicate or immediate as it might be via proper mechanical differentials, but it's still an impressive set-up. The ice stages on Sega Rally II were never this easy.

I simply can't tell you how incisive the Golf R's steering is – or how high the grip levels are – on asphalt. My guess would be that it'll prove a slightly softer and ultimately less exciting instrument than the very sharpest fast hatches, but it should be a more habitable and user-friendly one than most. Priced not so far from the considerably less engaging Golf GTI, though, it's a car I'd expect the hot hatchback fraternity to adopt in large numbers. This is a daily driver, not a track-day weapon for special occasions. But for all that, it's still a compelling drive.

MATT SAUNDERS

VOLKSWAGEN GOLF R	
Price	£29,900
0-62mph	5.1sec
Top speed	155mph
Power	296bhp at 5500-6200rpm
Torque	280lb ft at 1800-5500rpm
Gearbox	6-spd manual

Peugeot RCZ R

10.1.14, Coventry British roads hold no fear for Peugeot's most powerful production model to date, and make no mistake, it's a proper driver's car

FIRST VERDICT

Not quite the best front-driver around, but a damned good one

★★★★☆

SO GOOD

- Perfectly judged steering
- Bags of grip
- Taut but forgiving ride

NO GOOD

- Tiny back seats
- Fascia looks and feels antiquated
- Handling balance could be better

TESTER'S NOTE

Turn off the ESP and it stays off. Or leave it on: grip levels are so high that you'll hardly notice. MS

Front sports seats are covered in leather and Alcantara, but fascia is looking dated

THE PEUGEOT RCZ R couldn't arrive in UK showrooms at a better time. With a highly credible Volkswagen Golf rival now on the market in the shape of the new 308, the French car maker's reputational stock will be rising. Meanwhile, enthusiasts like you and me can only have been buoyed by last year's very respectable 208 GTI hot hatch. Some of us also vividly remember the incredible sight of a Peugeot obliterating the course record at Pikes Peak. Suddenly, anything looks possible from this company.

The new hot RCZ was built by the same people that made Sébastien Loeb's record-breaking hillclimber: the motorsport specialists at Peugeot Sport. This is the fastest and most powerful Peugeot production car

there's ever been, but when there seems to be another 'fastest and most powerful' every passing fortnight, we can set greater stall by the thoroughness of the engineering overhaul involved here. The RCZ R comes with wider tracks and rims, new, trick suspension pick-up points and wheel geometry, 380mm performance brake discs and a Torsen locking front differential.

Unlike some previous fast Peugeots, the RCZ R is no half-measure. And yet it proves quite civil and unimposing just bumbling along a British B-road. The ride is short and taut but seldom harsh – it's probably quieter than an entry-level RCZ on a big set of optional rims – and the damper tuning is excellent, allowing just enough

suppleness. The diff's torque-sensing talents mean you don't even know it's there most of the time. There's no camber reaction or wheel fight redolent of, say, a Mk1 Ford Focus RS to contend with.

There is, however, an abundance of steering feedback, thanks to the wider, stickier tyres and firmer springs and bushings. Whatever the causes, it's wonderful to find a new car with steering so simply done and expertly judged, ready to drag you into the driving experience by your fingertips.

The RCZ R's 266bhp turbocharged 1.6-litre engine is better revving beyond 5000rpm than trading mid-range blows with the torquier modern 2.0-litre turbos with which it must compete. Let it spin and this

engine makes the RCZ R feel seriously quick. Just not quite quick enough to keep up with, say, a BMW M135i; RCZ R buyers will need to understand that there are punchier options available for the money.

But there's little that combines such pace with quite so much poise and sporting thrill. The chassis shuns roll and grips very hard on turn-in. Mid-corner, you're aware that – just as in lesser RCZs – the front wheels of this car are the ones marking the limit of your speed. You'd say the car could be a smidge better balanced, and that the diff could act more aggressively on the overrun, giving those front wheels extra impetus to tuck in.

But through the middle and last stages of a bend, this car comes into

PEUGEOT RCZ R	
Price	£31,995
0-62mph	6.1sec
Top speed	155mph
Power	266bhp at 6000rpm
Torque	243lb ft at
	1900-5500rpm
Gearbox	6-spd manual

its own. On the road, the differential chimes in quite smoothly but ultimately lets you lay on power sooner, and in greater quantities, than you'd dare believe to begin with. There's little steering interference – just enough to let you know what's going on – and consistent lateral grip even in slippery conditions.

Peugeot has produced something really convincing here. A Renault Mégane RS has a bit more handling vigour and a Volkswagen Scirocco R is more refined and useable, but you won't need the commitment of an asphalt rally champion to see the case for chopping in your VW for a palpably more vivid driving experience with the RCZ R. It's what we'd do.

MATT SAUNDERS

Heavily revised suspension and a Torsen limited-slip diff help to give the RCZ R incisive handling and an abundance of steering feel

Seat Leon Cupra 265

10.2.14, Barcelona Is this a sportier and more affordable Volkswagen Golf GTI or a pale imitation?

5584 HVH

IT WAS RATHER easy to harbour a soft spot for the previous Seat Leon Cupra R. Sophisticated it wasn't. Or pretty. Or pleasant inside. Such niceties were left to the Volkswagen Golf GTI and Scirocco R. The Spaniard was just candidly quick and comparatively cheap. And with five doors only, practical, too.

The new version is something different. For a start, the 'R' is reserved for an all-wheel-drive, 300bhp-plus model that's coming later. The inflated standard Cupra range now includes a three-door model alongside the familiar five-door, both powered by Volkswagen Group's latest turbocharged 2.0-litre petrol engine in a choice of 261bhp and 276bhp guises – the latter making it the most powerful series-production car that Seat has (yet) built.

It's a likely candidate for the most sophisticated model that the brand has ever built, too. For the first time, every Cupra comes with a mechanical front differential lock to make sense of 258lb ft of torque from 1750rpm. The electrically powered steering rack is now variably toothed for progressively sharper reactions, while the fully independent, lowered suspension (no torsion bar here) comes equipped with adjustable dampers and there's the option of a six-speed DSG to go with the standard six-speed manual gearbox. Seat has even gone to the bother of adding a Cupra setting to the car's selectable drive profiles.

The design alterations are less significant. The '280' variant (the 276bhp model) gets a rear spoiler and prettier 19-inch alloy wheels to distinguish it, but the '265', with only the bigger air intakes and diffuser-effect rear skirt, threatens to blend into the crowd a little too well. Both are good looking, though – a handy inherited trait of the current Leon from which the previous Cupra did not benefit. That quality is even more noticeable inside, where Seat has only really had to lever in sports seats (optional buckets come later), splash aluminium on the pedals and fatten the steering wheel for suitable effect. →

FIRST VERDICT

The Leon Cupra is fitter, faster and just plain nicer than before

★★★★☆

SO GOOD

- Strong performance
- Superior ride quality
- Appropriately good looking
- Decent value

NO GOOD

- Capable rather than thrilling
- The one you want isn't coming

TESTER'S NOTE

Seat has removed the panel door from the dashboard cubbyhole. Good. It looked cheap. NC

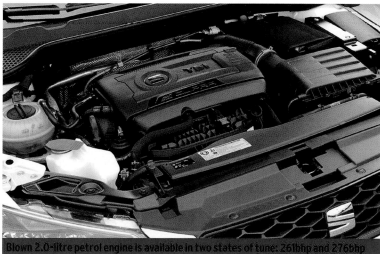

Blown 2.0-litre petrol engine is available in two states of tune: 261bhp and 276bhp

Leon Cupra handles with poise and a locking diff gives it a sticky nose, but adjustability is lacking

Cabin has more design appeal than its predecessor's; DSG auto 'box is optional and best avoided

The grown-up appeal oozing from the cabin is part of the reason why memories of the previous car – stiff, hollow-sounding job that it was – dissipate in moments. Instead, it's the Mk7 Golf GTI, the Cupra's pricier half-brother, that's brought to mind, and all too often humbled by the Latin upstart. Not just on the power front, either, although with plenty more of it and a claimed kerb weight of 1300kg, the Cupra is unquestionably faster than the GTI. Using a further evolution of the EA888 engine also found in the Golf R, its hard-edged, flat but phat delivery is typical of the series. Accessible and exploitable, if not electrifying, it comfortably sees the Leon in the upper echelons of the hot hatch mainstream.

That much could be gathered from the spec sheet. What certainly could not is how the car rides in its entry-level format. On 18-inch wheels and ContiSportContact 5s, the 265 flows along with considerably more élan than the Golf. In fact, on the admittedly accommodating Spanish autoroutes, the 265 variant positively glides, managing the trick of feeling immovably stable on lowered springs while ensuring that the rebound is considerably damped for better comfort – a characteristic that it retains even in the sterner settings available via the DCC system.

Cantankerous British surfacing may yet foil its high comfort levels, but south of Montserrat, the Leon is in Ford Focus ST territory. Or the 265 is, at any rate. The 19-inch wheels of the 280 do nibble away at the superlatives – not ruining the car by any means but certainly peeling away the top layer of compliance and replacing it with a bit more of a drone.

Fortunately, with wider Bridgestone Potenza RE050As at each corner, there's an obvious pay-off. With a reduced profile and better stickiness, the 280 enters, exits and transits between the two with more hard-bodied hustle than the 265. A to B on a plaster-smooth Spanish mountainside, bankrolled by the spry action of the six-speed manual (forget the outdated six-speed DSG), the 280 is unquestionably quicker on the limit.

Back in the real world, though, atop Blighty's varicose veins, there's

Smart sports seats are standard fit

It scrabbles to pull the nose around where the Golf GTI would settle for a slack dose of straight-ahead

every chance that you'd feel more comfortable going quicker in the more pliant 265. Especially given the conspicuous interaction of the new diff where traction is concerned. Borrowed from the Performance Pack-equipped Golf but retuned for the Cupra to deliver a much more industrious front end, it scrabbles to involve itself in pulling the nose around where the Golf GTI would settle for a slack dose of straight-ahead. Better still, it has all but eliminated any obvious torque steer.

Like everything else fused to the MQB platform, though, the Leon's chassis is short on gloss. Not accuracy, poise or punch, but there's too little to savour beyond its impassive and predictable grip. Beyond simply

forcing more torque through the diff, adjustability is in short supply.

Certainly, the Leon is keen for you to tuck it in and press on, but it assumes that a weight-shifting mid-corner step off the throttle is a wet-booted mistake rather than a deliberate request for deeper collaboration. The tame tuck of the rear end is a familiar trait – understandable and utterly dependable – but also the reason why the Focus ST and Renault Mégane RS 265 are rewarding in a way that the Leon Cupra can never be.

Such a shortcoming is easy to put into perspective, though. With this car's suppleness, Seat is hardly courting the hardcore hatch enthusiast. What it is interested in,

though – helped by 40mpg-plus claimed economy and CO_2 emissions of less than 160g/km – is courting the young-at-heart buyer who is chasing a bit of affordable all-round talent. In that respect, it has played something of a blinder with the new Cupra.

Or it would have done if the manufacturer had opted to import the five-door version of the 265, the car that best combines the Cupra's suppleness, pace and practicality. But it hasn't. If British buyers want five doors, they'll have to go for the more powerful but slightly less comfortable Cupra 280. Seat is betting that a greater proportion of buyers will opt for that version, and we wouldn't dissuade them necessarily, but at £27,240 the Leon is getting on for

serious money – and for all of its added maturity, the Cupra feels once again like a car best bought cheaply. At £25,690, the 265 is £435 less expensive than a basic three-door Golf GTI, making its Q-car looks, satisfying rapidity and contented ride something of a no-brainer for the right-minded hot hatchback connoisseur.
NIC CACKETT

SEAT LEON CUPRA 265	
Price	£25,690
0-62mph	5.9sec
Top speed	155mph
Power	261bhp at 6600rpm
Torque	258lb ft at 1750-5300rpm
Gearbox	6-spd manual

BMW i8

25.4.14, Los Angeles BMW breaks new ground
with its dramatic new plug-in hybrid sports car

FIRST VERDICT

**Extravagant, fluent, fast, frugal –
but lacking clarity of purpose**

★★★★☆

SO GOOD

- Torquey initial performance
- Steering and powertrain response
- 40mpg day-to-day fuel economy

NO GOOD

- A bit short on involvement
- Ultimate lack of supercar punch
- Synthesised engine noise

TESTER'S NOTE

The boot's not as big
as in a Porsche 911
or Audi R8, but rear
seat space adds lots
of practicality. **MS**

IT CAN BE misleading to classify a car primarily by the type of powertrain it has, rather than by the purpose it's designed to serve. So say enlightened, intelligent, experienced industry people. After a drive in the BMW i8, I'm inclined to agree.

The i8, says BMW, is the zen-like, sustainable, low-emissions, petrol-electric, 'new-premium' German sports car of the future. Expressions of concept don't get much more complicated than that. But although the two most important words in that string get crowded out by their louder neighbours, they are undoubtedly

'sports car'. Or rather, they should have been – written in bold, enlarged, indelible type.

Unfortunately, that isn't quite how it transpires. Because the i8 turns out to be a vehicle of incredible visual impact, laudably mature execution and a uniquely appealing ownership proposition among cars of its ilk. But to drive it isn't really to 'get' it or to acquaint yourself with the future of the sports car rather than it is experience a £100k BMW that might just be a tad too clever for its own good.

Although it serves as a flagship and symbol of BMW's new 'i' sub-brand,

the i8 has roots that pre-date BMW i. It was the Vision EfficientDynamics concept of 2009 that first mooted the idea of a new mid-engined headline BMW sports car.

The Vision EfficientDynamics had two electric motors, though, and a turbodiesel engine, and we guessed that it might sire a road car called the Z10 ED. It wasn't for another two years that the i8's even more exotic final specification was revealed in a concept car of the same name – with carbonfibre/aluminium construction and one fewer electric motors but a petrol engine mounted midships.

The i8's pure electric range is about 15 mile

Cockpit is driver-focused and BMW has been much more flamboyant than usual with its interior design themes

Butterfly doors only add to the i8's supercar-grade visual impact, which easily rivals that of any Lamborghini

The i8 is a plug-in hybrid sports car, then – a Porsche 918 Spyder done for a fifth of the outlay, you might say. A 1.5-litre, three-cylinder engine shared with the new Mini Cooper is cradled between its back wheels and has a higher specific output than any production combustion engine that BMW currently makes, feeding 228bhp and 236lb ft to the rear wheels via a six-speed ZF automatic gearbox. Between the front wheels is a 128bhp, 184lb ft 'hybrid synchronous' electric motor, which drives those front wheels through a two-speed automatic transmission.

And here's the clever bit. That electric motor and transmission, the 7.1kWh lithium-ion battery mounted where the car's transmission tunnel might otherwise be and the high-voltage power management systems add almost exactly 200kg to the i8. Relative to an aluminium or steel equivalent, says BMW, the carbonfibre-reinforced plastic monocoque saves exactly 200kg. So the car weighs in at 1540kg with fluids on board, which is less than a current Porsche 911 Turbo, never mind the 918. The two-speed gearbox, meanwhile, allows the electric motor

to operate at peak torque as the combustion engine passes 3700rpm in the lower intermediate gears, so as well as 357bhp, you really do get 420lb ft of mid-range thrust from this car at times. It feels like it, too.

Early impressions of the i8 are of nothing less than a fully fledged supercar. The body looks ridiculously low, wide and ground-hugging. The styling has smack-in-the-chops impact to rival a Lamborghini – and butterfly doors to be doubly sure.

You have to fold yourself into the cabin between a low roofline and a high, wide sill. And once you have,

the interior has no less a sense of occasion, with a sculptural, driver-focused dashboard, colourful LCD instruments, low-slung sports seats and an abundance of little features and touches that lift the ambience way above BMW's conservative norm.

So it talks the talk, the i8 – loud and clear. Walking the walk of something as pure as a 911 was always going to be the hard bit – and, sure enough, on handling precision and that final sliver of driver engagement, the BMW falls short of brilliance. But it's still good – it's almost there. Certainly good enough to consider the car an →

← amazing success within its own hyper-specialised niche.

Right up until you're looking for that critical last fraction of driver appeal, in fact, the i8 does almost everything right. Starting off in Comfort mode on its adaptive dampers and silent drive turning its front wheels, the i8 is comfortable and super-civilised around town. It's a bit choppy-riding occasionally, but not often. The steering is light but quietly feelsome, and performance is entirely decent in electric mode. Electric-only range is a bit mean in reality, though, at about 15 miles.

Knock the amber-illuminated gear selector into Sport mode and the engine begins to run almost continuously. Gun the accelerator away from a standstill and the powertrain feels like a big V6 through the mid-range: both instant and heavy-hitting on pedal response, with a loud, gruff, synthesised soundtrack broadcast to you over the audio speakers. And yet, the harder it revs and the faster you go, the smaller that imaginary V6 becomes. Indeed, work it really hard beyond the 5000rpm mark and the i8's performance level feels a touch thin and strained.

The car's handling stands up more stoutly to inspection – but not indefinitely. Body control is excellent and steering response equally immediate. Lateral grip levels could be higher, particularly at the front wheels, which begin to scrabble and scream under load if you harry them.

Drive intelligently, using weight transfer to give the steering authority on turn-in, and the i8 responds like any good mid-engined car should. The rear axle is always glued to its line, giving dependable stability, but it declines any attempt to adjust your cornering line using the throttle.

The upshot is that the i8 doesn't quite feel as exciting as it does fast. It's secure and fluent, but not the last word in fun. Accounting for its novelty value, brimming supercar attitude and its low-emissions sense of environmental responsibility, it'll be more than sporting enough to satisfy people who perhaps couldn't otherwise have justified a sports car.

But it's not quite convincing enough to hit the heights that true enthusiasts will expect. There is lots of intriguing complexity here, but sadly not quite enough depth.

MATT SAUNDERS

Laser headlights beam in

ALTHOUGH THE i8 comes with full LED headlights and tail-lights as standard, it becomes BMW's first production model to feature 'laser diode' lighting as an option. Besides being several times smaller and lighter than equivalent LEDs and three times more energy-efficient, laser lights can be guided much more precisely than LED beams and are 70 per cent brighter.

Actuated by BMW's camera-based High Beam Assistant system, the laser lights have a range of up to 600 metres – twice that of regular LEDs, it says.

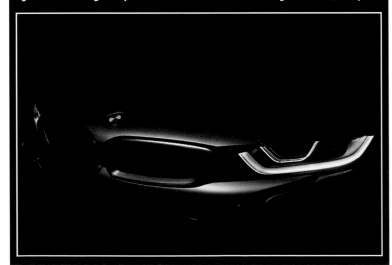

The i8's hybrid powertrain feels like a big V6 through the mid range: instant and heavy-hitting

BMW i8	
Price	£99,845 (excl £5k gov't grant)
0-62mph	4.4sec
Top speed	155mph
Power	357bhp at 5800rpm
Torque	420lb ft at 3700rpm
Gearbox	6-spd automatic (petrol),
	2-spd automatic (electric)

Jaguar XFR-S Sportbrake

Executive estate gets a supercharged V8 and a hefty dose of added horsepower

FIRST VERDICT

Fast, sharp-handling estate will be an impressive cross-country tool

★★★★☆

SO GOOD

- Mighty but cultured engine
- Body kit looks sharp
- Good driving position
- Estate-specific chassis tweaks

NO GOOD

- Easy to overwhelm rear wheels
- Boot capacity behind the best

TESTER'S NOTE

The steering is quite heavy at low speeds, but the weighting becomes ideal as the pace builds. HH

XFR-S Sportbrake's 502lb ft overwhelms the rear tyres with ease in slower corners

Lateral suspension stiffness is up by 30 per cent over the standard XF Sportbrake

THE XFR-S SPORTBRAKE is Jaguar's first high-performance estate. It is powered by the same 542bhp supercharged 5.0-litre V8 found in the potent XFR-S saloon.

The car's eight-speed automatic gearbox gets the new 'Quickshift' technology first seen on the F-type. This, says Jaguar, makes the transmission even quicker to respond, and it has a corner recognition function to choose the best possible ratio for exits.

Changes have also been made to the Sportbrake's rear suspension to handle the extra mass of the estate car body. Spring rates and lateral suspension stiffness are up 30 per cent over the standard XF. The adaptive damping, active electronic rear differential and Dynamic Stability Control settings have been tweaked for the estate, too.

Aside from an extravagant body kit (claimed to reduce lift while improving engine cooling by five per cent), the XFR-S is marked out by carbonfibre parts, carbonfibre-effect cabin trim and double-line stitching with 'micro-piping' on the leather. Load capacity is 1675 litres, although with the rear seats in place the boot is quite shallow beneath the load cover.

The cars we drove briefly on the narrow roads above Lake Geneva were still classed as pre-production prototypes, and we didn't have the time at the wheel – or the safety space on the road – to really stretch the car.

However, there's no doubt that the Sportbrake is a very different beast to Audi's RS Avant line. Unlike the increasingly refined and limo-like – if still devastatingly fast – Audis, the Jag is much more demonic.

Much of that demonism comes from sheer wallop. With the full 502lb ft available at just 2500rpm, it is amazingly easy to break traction. Rounding a near-180deg hairpin, just tapping in a little acceleration was enough to spin up the inside wheel.

In a straight line, the XFR-S was predictably rapid. Jaguar has emphasised the engine sound and the exhaust note, but within reason; it's there, but nicely in the background.

There's not much else we can definitively say after a short drive, except that the XFR-S is easy to place on the road, steers pretty accurately and feels well built. It also has a nice, meaty weight to the steering. The extra lateral stiffness of the suspension, along with the wide tyres, did mean that the car was prone to following the undulations of one badly surfaced road too closely, but overall the ride quality seemed well judged for a high-performance car.

The XFR-S Sportbrake is an interesting proposition. It is not as refined as the Audi RS models but is rather closer to the more precise, engineered flavour that AMG manages to instill in such cars as the Mercedes CLS Shooting Brake. The Jaguar also lacks the security of the RS models' all-wheel drive, making it closer to a pure sports car.

It's an unexpected combination of executive car and hard-edged driver's machine, and the right sort of driver will find the XKR-S a gloriously challenging cross-country racer. But in anything but perfect conditions, it will demand an attentive and skilled driver to extract its best. Buyers should be sure they want a car that demands this attention, rather than just a very powerful executive estate. **HILTON HOLLOWAY**

JAGUAR XFR-S SPORTBRAKE	
Price	£82,495
0-62mph	4.6sec
Top speed	186mph (limited)
Power	542bhp at 6500rpm
Torque	502lb ft at 2500-5500rpm
Gearbox	8-spd automatic

Porsche
Cayman GTS

7.5.14, Majorca Porsche's mid-engined coupé gets more power, less weight and honed dynamics

GO FOR A drive, long or short, in a Porsche Cayman S and if you are afflicted by the bug – if you get what this magazine chunters on about week in, week out – then you will climb out feeling somewhere between elated and gob-smacked.

Elated because what you will have experienced is a sports car that provides joy to its driver at pretty much every single rotation of its tyres; gob-smacked because there's a fair chance that you won't have experienced anything quite like it on four wheels ever before, so rich is the seam of communication between car and driver, so lovely is the Cayman S to drive.

Now Porsche has gone one better and given us the GTS version of its latest Cayman. And having driven it, having sampled first-hand how giddy this car can make you feel when you are going for it over a great road, I am struggling to find words to describe it.

You probably think that I'm going way over the top at this point. You might even think that I'm making it up, or that I've lost my grasp on reality, having been subjected to a constant pummelling of high g-forces and monumental horsepower over the past few weeks in the form of Ferrari's LaFerrari, the Lamborghini Huracán and the McLaren P1.

But don't fret: I haven't lost it. The Cayman GTS has brought me back down to earth, post-hypercar-fest, with a delicious kind of a whumpf, a bit like when you freefall face down into a giant duvet. And the landing has been, well, really rather well timed, to be honest, because I'm not joking when I say that the Cayman GTS could, at a pinch, be the most delightful car I've driven this year.

Why? Because it's more than fast enough, thanks, and the way in which it interacts with your hands and backside is, in its way, every bit as →

Alcantara-trimmed cabin gets Sport Chrono package as standard; PDK gearbox is an option, but manual is preferable in this car

In GTS form, the compact Cayman feels wonderfully responsive and connected, especially with the optional sports suspension

Torque vectoring and dynamic engine mounts

IN THE NEW Cayman GTS, you get Porsche's latest dynamic engine mounts and its torque vectoring system as standard, both of which were developed on the 911 Turbo. The engine mounts help reduce the effects of inertia over the rear axle when cornering so are vital to the heavier 911s, such as the Turbo, but add an extra hit of precision to the mid-engined Cayman. The torque vectoring aids turn-in and traction by tickling the brakes of the unloaded inside rear wheel when cornering, and it works. The GTS understeers slightly less than other Caymans and feels to have the traction of a limpet on the way out of corners.

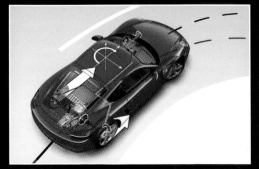

←incredible as anything a LaFerrari or a P1 can make you feel. Genuinely, the Cayman GTS is that good.

So what's different about the GTS compared with the regular old Cayman S? For starters, the power from its 3.4-litre flat six has risen gracefully to a rousing 336bhp, while its torque has also swollen, to 280lb ft. The sports exhaust becomes a standard fitment, too.

At the same time, the car's kerb weight has been trimmed to a feather-light 1345kg and, as a combination, this makes it a decent chunk quicker than the already pretty brisk S version. Think 0-62mph in 4.9sec with a manual gearbox or 4.6sec with the optional PDK and you get an idea of how rapid it has become.

Better still, though, is what

Porsche has done to the suspension. As standard, the GTS gets the once optional PASM and Sport Chrono packages, straight out of the showroom. But as a no-cost option, you can also choose something called the 'sports chassis', which does away with the electronic dampers and gives you traditional, analogue shock absorbers plus a further 10mm drop in ride height, the regular GTS already sitting 10mm lower than the S. And this is where the real gold doth lie.

Dial in some optional sports seats and, if you're feeling flush, the optional carbon-ceramic brake discs as well, and what you end up with is (a) the exact spec of the car that I drove on the launch, (b) the sweetest Cayman GTS combination it is possible to buy and (c) one of the most

PORSCHE CAYMAN GTS	
Price	£55,397
0-62mph	4.6sec
Top speed	177mph
Power	336bhp at 7400rpm
Torque	280lb ft at 6500rpm
Gearbox	6-spd manual

compelling driver's cars that sensible money has ever been able to buy.

You can pick a GTS from its lesser brethren outwardly, too, if you look closely enough. The light lenses are a couple of shades darker than normal, the light surrounds and lower spoiler at the front and valance at the rear

GTS is distinguished by a new front spoiler, 20-inch wheels and a lower ride height

are black and there are new 20-inch wheels. The whole lot also rides a little bit lower, which will always lend any car a certain edge.

The car that I drove had optional sports bucket seats, with fixed backs à la GT3, and although they made entry and egress a touch undainty,

once ensconced in them they felt fantastic. But it's the way that the Cayman GTS steers, rides, handles, stops, goes and sounds that will send you – and it – to another dimension.

There is a cohesion to the way that this car goes down the road that is rare, if not unique, in my experience. There are 911 fans who claim that the bigger car is still better to drive – that the Cayman remains its lieutenant, no matter what form it might take or how good it may be to drive. But I am no longer one of these people.

The Cayman GTS feels connected and compact and responsive to your inputs – be that via throttle, steering, brake pedal or gearlever, which slices quite beautifully up and down its six-speed gate – in a way that a 911 no longer does. The last time a regular 911

felt this alive and this keyed in to the part of your brain that revels in the art of driving was a very long time ago.

Indeed, you need to look to some fairly special versions of the 911 to match the satisfaction that the GTS Cayman provides – to the second-gen 996 GT3, perhaps, or the 997 GT3 RS and the current GT3. And this puts the Cayman GTS in very high company and me right out on a limb among Porsche's commentators, some of whom will take great offence at such heresy towards the sacred 911.

But, for me, that's how good the Cayman GTS with sports chassis, manual gearbox, carbon-ceramic brakes and sports seats feels. Which is some statement. But then the Cayman GTS really is some car.

STEVE SUTCLIFFE

POWER TO THE PEOPLE

Mass-market cars fight it out for the BTCC crown, but these racing machines are very different from their road-going counterparts, as **Matt James** explains

PHOTOGRAPHY STUART PRICE

Airwaves Racing Focus uses a Mountune-developed 2.0 turbo with 320-330bhp

The premise of the British Touring Car Championship is that it contains cars that trackside fans can relate to. A quick glance at the car park at Brands Hatch's opening rounds demonstrate the fact; the cars on the grid are the same models that people use in everyday life.

But the race machines themselves are the product of many thousands of man-hours and detailed reworking that is more usually associated with the very highest levels of motorsport.

Airwaves Racing is a multiple BTCC race-winning team, and it is likely to be a leading player in this season's competition because it has recruited double champion Fabrizio Giovanardi to handle its Ford Focus RS. The outfit is based just a few miles from the gates of Brands Hatch in Kent, and its headquarters are where the race machine takes shape. →

A road car has visual similarities with the racer, but little else

BTCC rules state that it must be 2.0 litres and turbocharged

'When dealing with racing cars, we go to a different level of precision'

Team manager Oly Collins explains: "Some teams might just buy a bodyshell, but we prefer to buy a complete road car and go from there, because there are several parts that we can carry over. Things like the door rubbers, some of the wiring loom, the light clusters, doors and bonnet will all come in useful for us later on.

"The first job is to strip the car back down to the bare bodyshell, and then we take it to be acid-dipped. We do this so that the paint is stripped away, and it also makes it a better surface to weld things to. The process also removes all the sealant from the other parts of the shell and other materials that are put in to soundproof the vehicle. It literally takes the car right back to the bare metal."

Sensors are sited all over the car to help the team set it up for race day

Once the car is returned to the team after this process, there is more refinement to be done before the hard work can begin on turning it into a race machine. More of the vehicle's basic features have to be removed.

"You have to de-bracket the entire donor car," says Collins. "We will remove the fixtures for the seatbelts, for example, and the roof lining. We will pare everything right back – and that has the benefit of lightening the vehicle as well."

Then the precision work starts. When a road car comes off the production line, the theory is that everything is identical. But in the motor racing world, where millimetres count, all measurements have to be double-checked.

"We will put the car on a jig, which has the precise measurements we want for the suspension pick-up points and things like that, because we need repeatability. Everything has to be exactly the same from race car to

Rear wing profile is determined by the NGTC regulations

Spot the difference: road car's familiar cabin is dismantled and largely discarded...

Then the cockpit is rebuilt with a roll cage, race seat, harness and electronic dash

race car," says Collins. "The road cars are generally very good in terms of being exact, but when you are dealing with racing cars, we go to a different level of precision."

Once the crew is satisfied that the car is to the exact dimensions that it requires, the first of the race-bred parts can begin to take shape.

The BTCC mandates a number of controlled parts, determined by the series organisers, which are common across all race machines. These are called the Next Generation Touring Car, or NGTC, rules (see sidebar on p81) and were introduced in 2011 to help curb the spiralling costs in tin-top competition in the UK.

Collins says: "We have to install the front and rear subframes, which are standard NGTC parts built by a firm called GPRM. We strip the bodyshell back to the bulkhead and then put the front subframe in, which will also have been on a jig to make sure that it is absolutely accurate. Things like this are vital, because a wrong measurement here will affect the handling of the entire machine. From there, we will add the suspension pick-up points to the front and rear subframes. Within reason, they have to be similar to the road car pick-up points to comply with the rules.

"There is an aerodynamic splitter that is attached to the front of the car, and where that fits on to the subframe dictates the height of the suspension pick-up points. You can't have it too low, otherwise you would fail the mandatory ride height tests executed after each of the on-track sessions."

After the suspension process is completed, the base of the fuel tank is welded into the car and the roll cage is installed – again, it is welded to the shell of the car. The machine is now beginning to take shape, and it has already taken two men six weeks and 1000 man-hours to get the nascent racer to this stage.

Airwaves Racing is one of the few operations on the BTCC grid to have its own in-house paint shop, so the car is then coloured in deference to the team's main backer.

"After the suspension work is done, we will install our engine, which is a Mountune-developed 2.0-litre turbocharged motor that puts out between 320bhp and 330bhp, and it is mated to a standard six-speed sequential Xtrac gearbox," explains Collins. "We put the suspension together, with the wishbones and the dampers, which are standard units from Penske. There are certain things that we can develop ourselves within the dampers, such as the shims and the valves, and we're also free to choose the springs. We use ones that are produced in Australia. Alongside the engine installation, there are certain bespoke parts that we can then put on the car, such as the fuel lines, oil lines, alternator and manifold. We can create certain parts, but they have to be homologated before the start of the season so that they remain the same for the rest of the year. →

"What is different from a road car is that we fit the car with a huge number of sensors, even on things like the suspension. That means we can monitor its movement and that helps us refine the handling over the course of a race weekend. That's something that is very important to us."

While the suspension is being bolted on, other engineers set to work installing the internals of the cockpit area of the car, including the racing seat and its six-point harness, as well as the highly complex electronic racing dashboard.

With the advent of turbocharging in the BTCC, one of the key areas that teams have had to work on is the cooling of the engine bay. It is a new issue that engineers have worked hard to figure out.

Collins says: "The intercooler that we use has a common core, but we are free to introduce any ducting that we want. In terms of the bodywork, we have a free hand to do what we want, but any designs that we have also have to be homologated ahead of the season. We have to submit an application to the series' technical officials ahead of the build process for them to approve it, and then that is also homologated and set in stone. While there are certain parts of the design process that are completely free-form, there is the provision in the rules for the series boss, Alan Gow, to say no to anything he might not like.

"There is an area that is 200mm below the bumper where we have a free hand in terms of the styling and that extends out to the edge of the front wings, which are wider than on a road car because the BTCC cars have to be built to a mandated width. The front grille has to resemble the scale and positioning of the road car."

The car is virtually completed now, with the regulation-controlled AP brakes fitted and the outside of the car stickered up to make it look like a proper racing thoroughbred. After a quick check on the flat patch to ensure that everything on the car is set exactly as it should be, the team is ready to

Fitting out the cockpit with such items as the seat and harness is one of the last jobs

NEXT GENERATION TOURING CAR REGULATIONS *AT A GLANCE*

CARS
Vehicles must be available to buy through a manufacturer's normal dealership network.

BODYSHELL
Two, three, four or five doors with a minimum length of 4.4m. Two-door and three-door shells are permitted as long as they share the same standard profile as the base model. Standard width is 1875mm.

ENGINES
Turbocharged 2.0-litre. Can be sourced from the maker's family range, including subsidiary firms.

FUEL TANK
80 litres.

TRANSMISSION
Front-drive or rear-drive only.

CLUTCH
AP Racing, carbon.

BRAKES
AP Racing package and pedal box.

THROTTLE
Fly by wire.

ELECTRONICS
Cosworth electronics, incorporating ECU, dash and data logger. Common wiring loom.

SUSPENSION
Mandated front subframe to incorporate suspension, brakes, transmission and engine location. Standard rear subframe. Adjustable double wishbone suspension with coilover dampers.

GEARBOX
Xtrac six-speed sequential.

WHEELS
18-inch, centre-locked.

AERODYNAMICS
Specified front aerodynamics, including flat floor, opening for the radiator, brake cooling, intercooler and side exits. Specified wing profile.

load the car into the truck and head off to the racing circuits.

Collins says: "By the time we have completed everything, including buying the mandated parts, the component cost alone can be in the region of £200,000. To get everything together usually takes up to five months, but we managed to do a complete car in seven weeks in 2012 because that was our self-imposed deadline. That was during the middle of a season, though, which meant there was less demand on the parts suppliers. Including the man-hours involved in creating the car, you are looking at between £220,000 to £240,000. It is a long way from your average family hatchback..." **A**

SIDEWAYS CHALLENGE
HERE COMES

ASTON MARTIN RAPIDE

ALPINA D3 BITURBO

JAGUAR F-TYPE V6 S

LOTUS EVORA S

SUBARU BRZ

THE FUN

Be it art, science or mindless mucking about, driving sideways is an awful lot of fun. But which car is best for a spot of drifting? **Matt Prior** decides

PHOTOGRAPHY STUART PRICE & AL STALEY

MERCEDES-BENZ C63 AMG COUPE

MAZDA MX-5 GT

AUDI R8 4.2 FSI

PORSCHE 911 GT3

911 GB

"I'll crash over there; you film it"

Group nonchalance hides pre-event tensions

Pre-run thousand-yard stares are de rigueur

Car scoring is done with Prior at the wheel

PORSCHE 911 GT3

Price	£100,540
Power	468bhp
Layout	Rear-engined, RWD, limited-slip differential
Peak drift angle	48deg at 14.9mph
Average g	0.37g
Average speed	20.3mph
Total score	13.97

Trying to justify it is tempting. It's tempting, too, to pretend to be worthy and conscientious and suggest that the assessment of transient dynamic behaviour over the next few pages is, in fact, crucial to overall objective handling tests.

It is, I suppose, but that's not why it started. The Sideways Challenge existed in the first instance – and has been resurrected now – simply because everybody involved in the doing and the reading of it thought it was a right old giggle.

So here we are, on one of Oulton Park's two rally stages – a low-grip drift circuit, to you and me – with nine of the UK's most sideways cars. And, in a few pages' time, once we've decided which is our most driftable car, we have nine people who each think they might be Britain's most sideways driver.

First, though, to the cars. We've brought them along because we think they'll excel at going sideways. Most follow the mechanical convention you'd expect for producing bags of controllable oversteer: an engine in the front and rear-wheel drive.

In no particular order, those cars are the Jaguar F-type V6 S, the Alpina D3 Biturbo, the Aston Martin Rapide, the limited-edition Mazda MX-5 GT, the Subaru BRZ (this test wouldn't be complete without a BRZ or a Toyota GT86, and the Toyota usually gets the limelight) and the Mercedes-Benz C63 AMG coupé in Edition 507 form.

All of these cars are equipped with a limited-slip differential, which should eliminate any tendency to merely spin power away through an inside wheel and instead send the cars pleasingly sideways.

And then there are the outsiders. Lotus's Evora is a mid-engined, rear-wheel-drive junior supercar. We know from experience that it will go sideways, and do so very controllably, but with an open differential we suspect it will be trickier to control than the front-engined cars.

Ditto the Audi R8, we think. This is four-wheel drive, albeit with the power mostly going to the all-important rear pair of wheels, via a limited-slip differential. Again, we know it will go sideways, but we are expecting it to be difficult to give it the appropriate 'send'.

Finally, there's Porsche's 911, in nothing less than GT3 specification, which brings with it very firm suspension, tyres that are at their happiest in dry conditions (which are conspicuous by their absence) and an engine that, as ever, hangs out →

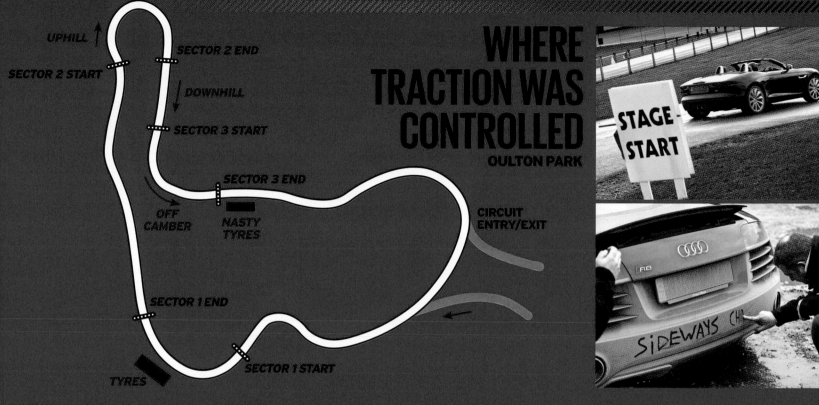

UPHILL ↑

SECTOR 2 END

SECTOR 2 START

↓ DOWNHILL

SECTOR 3 START

SECTOR 3 END

OFF CAMBER

NASTY TYRES

CIRCUIT ENTRY/EXIT

SECTOR 1 END

SECTOR 1 START

TYRES

WHERE TRACTION WAS CONTROLLED
OULTON PARK

STAGE START

SIDEWAYS CHA

OULTON PARK IS a cracking track, but not entirely suitable for the job at hand. Fortunately, it also has two asphalt rally stages – one flat and one with plenty of gradient, which we used.

They're curious little tracks, because the grip levels are already low. Throw in some rain (and a bowser in case the sun came out) and you end up with highly entertaining limits of adhesion and power oversteer in cars that would usually struggle to push sideways on the throttle alone. And all without the pebble-dashing you'd get from a gravel surface and minus the tyre squeal (which is a bigger issue than engine noise at most circuits) and tyre wear problems.

In previous Sideways Challenges, we've used judges, but this time we wanted some hard data. Step forward the Racelogic DriftBox, which measures the slip angle and can assign a score to it, thus deciding what is a 'good' drift and what is a 'bad' one. Not all competitors liked it, but it was the same for every driver and every car. Basically, if you go a long way sideways and pull it back, you'll get a good score. But if you stop or spin, it stops counting. If you stop drifting, it stops counting. Because of this, we divided the circuit into three corners, each navigable in a single, long drift. Speed, average drift angle and peak drift angle all form part of the score.

ALPINA D3 BITURBO	
Price	£46,950
Power	345bhp
Layout	Front-engined, RWD, limited-slip differential
Peak drift angle	35deg at 14.9mph
Average g	0.37g
Average speed	20.36mph
Total score	13.09

LOTUS EVORA S

Price	£62,290
Power	345bhp
Layout	Mid-engined, RWD, open differential
Peak drift angle	36deg at 15.3mph
Average g	0.39g
Average speed	20.7mph
Total score	13.5

JAGUAR F-TYPE V6 S

Price	£60,235
Power	375bhp
Layout	Front-engined, RWD, limited-slip differential
Peak drift angle	44deg at 14.9mph
Average g	0.37g
Average speed	19.9mph
Total score	14.37

SUBARU BRZ SE	
Price	£24,995
Power	197bhp
Layout	Front-engined, RWD, limited-slip differential
Peak drift angle	32deg at 21.7mph
Average g	0.46g
Average speed	22.2mph
Total score	13.06

←behind the rear axle, for maximum pendulous effect. It should be the trickiest of the lot to control. This, then, could go one of two ways.

And to measure it all, we've got a Racelogic DriftBox, an ingenious piece of hardware that uses global positioning to determine a car's speed and direction, plus internal accelerometers to calculate its angle of attack around any given corner.

Because of the distinctly complicated way the DriftBox works, we've divided our circuit into three sections rather than taking it as a whole. The DriftBox will measure the peak drift or slip angle as well as the speed at which it occurred. It will also note the average g-force and average speed through the corner and then it'll happily package all of these and display them as an overall score for each section, a bit like an Olympic ice skating judge. The higher the number, the better the score.

For consistency, I'll be at the wheel every time, giving each car the same number of laps (three, to be specific), taking the best score from each section and adding them all together. The winner is the one with the highest overall number. Simple.

Or so you'd think. Trouble is, this circuit has a low-grip surface at the best of times and it's wet when we arrive (there's a water bowser in case it looks like drying). My first two runs in a control car – one not in the contest – result in comedy low-speed rotations. Consider that, around a normal race track, in the dry, a sports car will typically pull 1g of lateral grip. On a wet race track, that might drop to 0.7, perhaps 0.8g. On Oulton's rally stage, the numbers the DriftBox returns are half that again. So I choose something that ought to be easy to control: Jaguar's F-type, which I know well because it's our long-termer. My long-termer, even.

And sure enough, the F-type is, once you've adjusted to the comically low limits, a very happy car when it's sideways. The throttle response is rapid and the diff hooks up quickly, so it's quick to break traction but easy to modulate when it does. It steers lightly and easily, too, and even though it wants a change from second to third gear halfway through the first corner, you can shift on a steering wheel paddle with no drama. The total score of 14.37 is one I think will be tough to beat.

Next, the Lotus Evora. Because of its open differential, it requires a much bigger prod to get its rear moving. But while I can think of a dozen mid-engined cars that scare the heck out of you when they start sliding, the Lotus has a vast amount of lock and nicely geared steering, while its natural drift angle – the one it most likes to adopt – is not near the lockstops. It also has, thanks to somebody's insistence at the design stage that it needed to be a 2+2, a long wheelbase, so there's a pleasingly broad playspace between going a little sideways and the point where it spins. It will spin if you let it, but an overall score of 13.5 means it's not as sideways a car as the Jaguar. No surprise there.

What is surprising are the performances of the next two. The Mazda MX-5 GT is wonderful at going sideways, despite a paucity of low-end grunt that means it usually wants to be in first gear. It is, however all but unspinnable and has the best steering here. Subaru's BRZ is a similarly easy car in which to go sideways. Both are immense fun, but because of the easily metered power and the fact that there isn't a great deal of it, what feels like a wonderfully fluid run in each car doesn't result in a great score. The DriftBox likes, it transpires, cars that adopt a big angle before coming back from it, not consistent drift machines such as these. The Mazda scores just 12.01, the BRZ 13.06. But if you had to pick a machine to take out just for fun, these two would be near the top of your list.

Also wanting first gear is the Audi R8. In second gear, too little torque →

AUDI R8 4.2 FSI

Price	£92,710
Power	424bhp
Layout	Mid-engined, 4WD, limited-slip rear differential
Peak drift angle	51deg at 15.4mph
Average g	0.37g
Average speed	20.4mph
Total score	15.64

ASTON MARTIN RAPIDE

Price	£149,995
Power	550bhp
Layout	Front-engined, RWD, limited-slip differential
Peak drift angle	32deg at 16.2mph
Average g	0.43g
Average speed	21.2mph
Total score	13.84

Off-track excursions were surprisingly few and far between

← reaches the rear wheels, so it understeers. Instead, it wants a prod in first, then a quick lift to quell the momentum of the mid-mounted engine, followed by getting back on the throttle and riding out the slide. It's easy to get that wrong and spin harmlessly, but get it right and the R8 will recover from a big angle and then, being four-wheel drive, pick up speed quickly and drive out of a corner with confidence.

It's not an easy car to drive this way, but there's no arguing with the numbers. The R8 achieves a huge recoverable drift angle, at 51deg off the straight ahead (most peaks start with a '2' or '3'), which is why it posts a total of 15.64.

I expect the Aston Rapide to be easy to drift (and it is), but it doesn't produce a mammoth score. With a vast wheelbase and a lazy throttle response at low revs, it takes a severe input to get it sideways, but there's all the time in the world to catch it. It also steers very naturally. The result is a score of 13.84, which is better than the Alpina's 13.09, and that despite the D3's more immediate low-end throttle response (although it hangs a little on lift-off) and a differential that hooks up cleanly.

The C63 AMG arrived in Edition 507 spec, which takes some getting

MAZDA MX-5 GT

Price	£29,995
Power	203bhp
Layout	Front-engined, RWD, limited-slip differential
Peak drift angle	30deg at 16.3mph
Average g	0.44g
Average speed	21.9mph
Total score	12.01

used to. It has what feels much like low-rev engine lag, or a differential that isn't hooking up cleanly. Either way, its tail doesn't let go very easily, but when it does, it wants big throttle inputs to keep it sideways. That said, the C63 is approachable, manageable and controllable, and an impressive score of 14.94 puts it above everything apart from the Audi R8.

Which just leaves the Porsche. And that wants a deep breath and a lot of patience, because it's remarkably

easy to put it into a spin once you get that pendulum effect going. Better, then, rather than giving it a send or a bung, to just gently push through any initial understeer and use the engine to shove the car around a bend with a little lock applied, rather than letting the motor pull the car around. It's a decent physics lesson, but things were ever thus in 911s and a score of 13.97 is no bad result – thanks largely to the recovery of a 48deg angle around the sector two hairpin.

But the 911's performance doesn't touch the top three: the lively Jaguar F-type in third, the challenging but ultimately trustworthy C63 AMG in second and, in first place (and something we didn't expect at all), Audi's hard to master but undeniably capable and impressive R8.

So Britain's most sideways car has got four-wheel drive and its engine in its middle. Who'd have thought it? Read on and we'll hand over the top two cars to our hired goons. →

MERCEDES-BENZ C63 AMG EDITION 507 COUPE

Price	£68,160
Power	500bhp
Layout	Front-engined, RWD, limited-slip differential
Peak drift angle	35deg at 16.9mph
Average g	0.44g
Average speed	21.8mph
Total score	14.94

MEET THE DRIFTERS

With our most driftable cars decided, it's time to inject some ego into proceedings. Who will be Autocar's Sideways Challenge champion? **Matt Saunders** adjudicates

This is where things get competitive. It's also where the Sideways Challenge has a bit of history. Previous events have focused solely on pitting well known drivers from the worlds of motorsport, chassis development and road testing against each other and hoping they wouldn't write anything off. Typically, of course, they did.

This time, as you've read, we'd make the drivers play second fiddle to the cars. You can imagine how well that went down. It was a miracle anyone showed up at all.

Invites went out like Willy Wonka's golden tickets, and ultimately nine brave men showed up at a wintery Oulton Park. Not entirely by accident, they represented a broad spread of motor industry specialisms and skill sets. Former Sideways Challenge champ and Lotus chassis guru Gavan Kershaw sent his apologies. Autocar's honour, meanwhile, would be defended by one S Sutcliffe.

For a while, we considered inviting the formerly-of-this-parish Mr Chris Harris, which would have been fun for everyone except yours truly, who had to ensure the day ran smoothly.

Unfortunately for Chris, however, our first choice Harris (Graham, tyre tester for Dunlop) was free and willing. Sorry, Monkey.

Our intrepid helmsmen would, like the cars, face trial by Racelogic DriftBox. Everyone would get three warm-up laps and one scored lap per round. There would be two rounds: first, a run in the Mercedes C63 AMG coupé (if you couldn't drift that, you shouldn't have turned up), then a trickier run in the four-wheel-drive, mid-engined Audi R8.

The datalogger would rate each driver's performance through each

of the three corners on Oulton's rally stage, before combining them to produce an an overall score. Spins automatically voided your score for the corner in question.

Experience suggested that, on the day and on the rally stage's surface in particular, a mark of seven was very good indeed for any single corner. Not many would get a seven, or even close to it. Plenty argued that the scoring system was unsophisticated, but we liked it because it wasn't vulnerable to the bribery, corruption, brow-beating, interpretation or human error that have come into play at previous →

1st

Darren Turner
Factory racing driver in the FIA World Endurance Championship with Aston Martin Racing

Relevant experience
Knocking on a decade in front-engined Aston GT sportscars. Often at night and in the wet, which should help here.

Judges' comments
First to figure out how to score highly; good enough not to tell everyone else straight away. Great company, top bloke, evidently very handy indeed. A worthy winner.

In his own words
"I don't know if that's how you're supposed to drive a C-class, but I really enjoyed it. I was off left, right and centre on my practice laps but got it together in the end. My heart was pounding, though – worse than in qualifying!"

Round one score
Mercedes-Benz C63 AMG, 17.62

Round two score
Audi R8 4.2 FSI, 16.32

Total score 33.94

Best single drift score 6.27, round one, corner two (41deg average drift angle)

Most sideways point 40.9deg, 16.2mph, round one, corner two

← Sideways Challenges. Basically, we thought the DriftBox might rule out argument. Fat chance.

So proceedings kick off in the AMG, with drivers waiting as patiently for their turn as six-year-olds queueing for the dodgems. The good-natured banter from the viewing area flows mainly from Sutcliffe, World Endurance Championship ace Darren Turner and BTCC driver Rob Austin, while quiet, steely confidence emanates from the likes of Graham Harris, former world record holder for the world's longest drift Mauro Calo and Jaguar Land Rover chassis man John Barker. Younger lads Michael Meadows (the back-to-back Porsche Carrera Cup champ), World Rally Championship driver Elfyn Evans and GP2 man and F1 reserve driver James Calado do their best to look like they have an idea of how well they might do and what they might say to excuse the damage and havoc they may well be about to cause.

Sutcliffe is first in the car, looking good and scoring quite well. Touring car driver Rob Austin runs next and duly outscores him, although he manages to introduce the C63 to the circuit's cones a couple of times, albeit not during his scoring lap.

Tyre tester Harris runs early, too, and sets what looks like an unbeatable score by almost spinning on corner three but saving the C63 from stopping dead by the skin of his teeth. Much muttering follows. Should a near-miss produce such a high score? Probably not, but rules is rules, we say.

The only man who actually spins the C-class on a scoring lap is Michael Meadows, on the hairpin at corner two. Stalling the car in the process means returning to the pits to reset the timing gear and ESP – so he ends up getting another attempt at the two remaining corners. But that second bite at the cherry isn't enough for him to score particularly highly overall.

Endurance racer Turner keeps his powder dry until late in the order. His 'slow in, fast out' method uses first gear to get as much slip angle and rate of acceleration as possible in a bend before seeing where he ends up. It works out well, the Le Mans class winner topping the leaderboard. →

Not everyone was happy with the scoring system, but some used it to their advantage

Everyone gets a second crack at scoring at the wheel of the R8 – but one man declines to take it. Evidently disgusted at his performance in the AMG, James Calado makes his apologies at lunchtime and leaves us. Luckily, everyone else is having too much fun to follow suit.

There are two spinners in round two, but it could have been more when you consider how spinnable a mid-engined sports car should be on a surface akin to compacted snow. Graham Harris had never driven a four-wheel-drive supercar before and neither had Elfyn Evans, and both perform not-so-neat 180s. However, Rob Austin and John Barker also struggle with the Audi, failing to be aggressive enough with off-throttle steering inputs to kick the car into the beginning of a long slide. It's a case of damned if you do, damned if you don't with the R8.

Scoring highest in the Audi are Messrs Turner (whose superlative car control proves to be no fluke), Sutcliffe (who just drives the R8 as he would on his way to the local shops) and Meadows (who shows his affinity with a rearward weight bias gleaned from racing 911s, as well as an ability to learn very quickly).

In the final reckoning, the easy consistency of stunt driver and drift specialist Mauro Calo wins him a

---

2nd

Steve Sutcliffe
Autocar editor-at-large

Relevant experience
Lots. See every other cornering shot published in Autocar since the late 1980s and most videos on autocar.co.uk. Has won these events before.

Judges' comments
Unerringly cool and consistent. Didn't get close to a spin. Complained that the competition wasn't tougher. Annoyingly talented.

In his own words
"With so many great drivers here, I'm delighted. I'm obviously available for WRC, BTCC or Carrera Cup drives any time."

Round one score
Mercedes-Benz C63 AMG, 11.65

Round two score
Audi R8 4.2 FSI, 15.07

Total score 26.72

Best single drift score 5.32, round two, corner one (33deg average drift angle)

Most sideways point 36.8deg, 16.2mph, round two, corner two

3rd

Mauro Calo
Stunt driver, wheelman for hire, ex-drift world record holder

Relevant experience
Until recently, the world record holder for the longest production car drift. Skids for money, mostly anonymously on a popular BBC TV motoring programme.

Judges' comments
Handled the Merc like it was his own (which it might as well have been). Handled the occasion even more gracefully. Competitive without really trying.

In his own words
"Loved the AMG, but I seemed to do better in the Audi. Track was a lot slipperier than I expected. Both runs felt good, though."

Round one score
Mercedes-Benz C63 AMG, 13.6

Round two score
Audi R8 4.2 FSI, 11.27

Total score 24.87

Best single drift score 5.13, round one, corner three (36deg average drift angle)

Most sideways point 39.8deg, 27.7mph, round one, corner three

---

4th

Graham Harris
Dunlop tyre tester

Relevant experience
More track time than most of us have desk time, plenty of it on similarly low-grip surfaces. A scary level of consistency at the wheel is all part of the job.

Judges' comments
Outstanding in the Mercedes but by his own admission struggled in the Audi due to unfamiliarity with 4WD. A quiet man, but one with seriously impressive car control.

In his own words
"The cars were fantastic. Getting the power down in the C63 was hard; the R8 was grippier but more snappy. Great fun."

Round one score
Mercedes-Benz C63 AMG, 17.02

Round two score
Audi R8 4.2 FSI, 6.46

Total score 23.48

Best single drift score 6.26, round one, corner three (64deg average drift angle)

Most sideways point 69.7deg, 13.5mph, round one, corner three

---

5th

Elfyn Evans
World Rally Championship driver with M-Sport

Relevant experience
Used to going sideways but typically on the loose. Used to 4WD, but not in mid-engined V8s. Aged 25, so only just old enough to go on Autocar's insurance.

Judges' comments
As committed as you'd expect and super-impressive for a youngster. Wasn't used to having to turn the ESP off. A spin in the R8 cost him a podium finish.

In his own words
"Very slippery out there, very challenging in both cars. Possibly harder in the Audi because you need to react more quickly."

Round one score
Mercedes-Benz C63 AMG, 13.04

Round two score
Audi R8 4.2 FSI, 9.57

Total score 22.61

Best single drift score 5.7, round one, corner two (37deg average drift angle)

Most sideways point 36.6deg, 17.3mph, round one, corner two

---

podium spot above some seriously talented and competitive rivals and behind our very own Steve Sutcliffe, who never put a foot wrong all day and always looked like he had plenty of skill in reserve.

But not even Sutcliffe did enough to usurp 2014 Sideways Challenge champion Darren Turner from the top spot, his combined score placing him firmly in a league of one. However you choose to splice and dice the DriftBox data – and even if you'd have thrown the timing gear away and judged the day entirely subjectively – Turner's superiority was unquestionable. Sickening, yes, but absolutely incontestable all the same. ◮

Audi's mid-engined, AWD R8 is officially (and surprisingly) Autocar's most sideways car, but it wasn't easy to get the best out of it

6th

John Barker
Chassis development engineer, Jaguar Land Rover

Relevant experience
See every other cornering shot published in Evo magazine since issue one. Now works alongside the notoriously unsideways Mike Cross at Jaguar Land Rover.

Judges' comments
Almost as unfazed as Sutcliffe – and similarly disgruntled about the scoring regime. Effortlessly precise. Should have been more aggressive in the R8.

In his own words
"AMG had just enough power, but I'm used to more. Both runs seemed sideways from inside. More chances to spin the R8."

Round one score
Mercedes-Benz C63 AMG, 13.65

Round two score
Audi R8 4.2 FSI, 8.67

Total score 22.32

Best single drift score 6.05, round one, corner two (39deg average drift angle)

Most sideways point 39.2deg, 16.1mph, round one, corner two

7th

Rob Austin
Driver and team owner, WIX Racing, British Touring Car Championship

Relevant experience
Surviving among the axe murderers of the BTCC, where just keeping your car on track routinely means hitting the lock stops.

Judges' comments
The class joker; great fun. Rob would still be there now, rotating in the Audi, if we'd have let him keep the keys. His lap in the Merc was determined, to say the least.

In his own words
"Apparently I'm not very good at this. Brushed some tyres in the Audi, even. I clearly need more practice!"

Round one score
Mercedes-Benz C63 AMG, 12.99

Round two score
Audi R8 4.2 FSI, 7.1

Total score 20.09

Best single drift score 5.13, round one, corner two (30deg average drift angle)

Most sideways point 41.6deg, 25.2mph, round one, corner three

8th

Michael Meadows
Two-time and reigning Porsche Carrera Cup GB champion

Relevant experience
Four seasons racing Porsches, plus stints in single-seaters and GT cars beforehand. Won every 'rising star' award going. Only a year older than young Elfyn.

Judges' comments
Didn't start well and was the only bloke who managed to spin the AMG. Engine in the wrong place, probably. Third-best score in the Audi, though.

In his own words
"Loads of power but little grip in the AMG. R8 was more to my liking. Hard convincing yourself sideways is best. Glad I came."

Round one score
Mercedes-Benz C63 AMG, 4.64

Round two score
Audi R8 4.2 FSI, 13.16

Total score 17.8

Best single drift score 4.91, round two, corner one (31deg average drift angle)

Most sideways point 38.2deg, 19.4mph, round two, corner three

9th

James Calado
GP2 driver with ART GP; Formula 1 reserve driver for Sahara Force India

Relevant experience
Youngest man in the field. Beat Buemi, Alguersuari and Vergne in karts. Went on, via Formula Renault, F3, GP3 and GP2, to Formula 1.

Judges' comments
Typical F1 driver wanted to change the format to 'who's quickest'. Went home instead of contesting round two – but was second last by that point already.

In his own words
"Totally opposite to what I'm used to doing. C-class was nicer car to drive, but the day was all about having fun for me."

Round one score
Mercedes-Benz C63 AMG, 10.05

Round two score
Audi R8 4.2 FSI, DNS

Total score 10.05

Best single drift score 3.77, round one, corner three (39deg average drift angle)

Most sideways point 39.7deg, 25.2mph, round one, corner three

THE BEST VIDEOS OF THE YEAR

Millions of you watched videos on autocar.co.uk in 2014. **Mark Tisshaw** revisits the most-viewed

WATCH

Tesla Model S vs Aston Martin Rapide S

The Tesla Model S is the future... today. It offers most of the usability of the world's best luxury saloons, but with no tailpipe emissions and a fraction of the running costs. And it properly handles. But can it beat the £150,000 Rapide S?

WATCH

LaFerrari – Maranello's new 950bhp masterpiece

The new LaFerrari is a staggeringly rapid hypercar that makes devastating use of its hybrid powertrain. But is it purely a technical tour de force, or a real driver's car, too? We head to Ferrari's Fiorano test track to find out.

WATCH

McLaren P1: exclusive on-track review

The P1 hybrid hypercar is the most advanced road car McLaren has ever built, but is it also entertaining? We put the P1 to the test on the road and at the Bahrain International Circuit to deliver the most in-depth video review available.

WATCH

Is Porsche's 918 Spyder better than a Bugatti Veyron?

Will a £650,000 hypercar feel too intimidating and edgy to drive at ten-tenths? We find out and ask whether this new generation of hypercars can match the previously undisputed hypercar king, the Bugatti Veyron.

How much power does a Tesla Model S produce?

We've declared the Model S a landmark car, but now it's time to see just how much power that electric motor makes. Will it shame some of the world's most exotic super-saloons? We strap the luxury EV to a rolling road to find out.

Porsche Macan vs Range Rover Evoque

Porsche purists might not like it, but the Macan is already a smash hit. It's easy to feel sorry for the Range Rover Evoque, but even the 46mpg Macan S Diesel trumps the baby Rangie when it comes to performance, ride and handling.

Ferrari F12 vs Porsche 911 Turbo S vs Mercedes SLS

This is the ultimate test of the latest and best supercars. Can the astonishing traction of the 552bhp 911 Turbo S compensate for its power shortfall versus the 622bhp and 731bhp offered by the SLS AMG Black Series and Ferrari F12?

McLaren 12C vs Ducati 1199 Panigale S

The Ducati 1199 Panigale S is a mould-breaking superbike, but how will it fare against one of our favourite supercars? Will the Panigale's epic power-to-weight ratio rule, or will the 12C's outright bhp win? We head to Cadwell Park to find out.

Alfa Romeo 4C vs Toyota GT86 vs Porsche Cayman

The new Alfa 4C has the right credentials for a winning sports coupé, but can it really rival the indomitable and similar-priced Porsche Cayman? Or how about the cheaper but highly entertainingToyota GT86? We take all three to the track

Is the new Mercedes C-class the best compact exec?

The new Mercedes-Benz C-class faces tough competition from the likes of BMW's 3-series and the Audi A4. It's a little larger yet up to 100kg lighter than the car it replaces, but is it now the most enjoyable compact executive to drive?

PEUGEOT'S PEKIN

A resurgent Peugeot unveiled this striking new five-door luxury car concept at the 2

PHOTOGRAPHY STUART PRICE

Hands whirling out before her, eyes fixed on mine, words quickening, Sophie Gazeau, colour and materials stylist for the Peugeot Exalt concept that you see before you, is hitting her stride: "There is more than one way to do luxury. A top-end leather handbag that has aged is more highly prized than one that has come straight out of the shop. Wooden furniture that has marked through use is said to have character. We hear a lot about authenticity, but what is authentic about a piece of wood that has 1000 layers of lacquer on it, or real

leather that is treated so much that it looks like plastic no matter for how many years you use it?"

Her passion runs deep, but so would yours if you'd battled through intense internal design competitions to earn the right to lead the direction of one of Peugeot's most important concept cars in recent years. The Exalt is more than an alternative take on the five-door luxury car. It is both a symbol of the rebirth of the brand and a steer on what the firm sees as a gilt-edged opportunity to establish itself in the lucrative luxury car market. And don't snigger at that

last statement; the fact that it was on display at the 2014 Beijing motor show was no coincidence, because Peugeot is well established in China, and Asian car buyers are known for being ready to embrace new ideas.

That Peugeot bosses sense opportunity should be no surprise. The company entered the Chinese car market as early as 1985, and although that joint venture faltered, a second initiative kicked off in 1992 with Dongfeng, which is now China's second-largest car maker and, in a twist of fate, a major shareholder in PSA Peugeot-Citroën following

its recent financial struggles. The benefits of a strident premium brand have already been reaped via Citroën's DS arm, which is enjoying stratospheric success among Chinese buyers. Now Peugeot wants in on the sales act and, most important, the profit margins that follow. Brilliantly – and beautifully – it also has the confidence to realise it must achieve its goal by offering an alternative to what's already out there.

This 4.7m-long saloon-cum-hatch, with its unusually low roofline of just 1.31m, is meant to grab your attention for far more than just its innovative

PANAMERA

...ijing motor show. **Jim Holder** finds out what makes the Exalt so significant

Gilles Vidal and Sophie Gazeau

looks. A plug-in hybrid, it has the same 1.6 THP engine that powers the RCZ R, but the four-pot petrol engine's 266bhp is supplemented by a 67bhp electric motor that's mounted on the multi-link rear axle. It is built on a version of the EMP2 platform that underpins the new generation of PSA cars, including the Car of the Year-winning Peugeot 308. All good stories, you'd think. But in almost four hours with the car and a succession of interviews with five of its creators, not one of them mentions either its powertrain or platform, which gives a sense of the project's priorities.

"We spent 18 months creating this concept, at least six months longer than usual for a concept car," says Gilles Vidal, Peugeot's style director. "The body shape and proportions are especially complex, and we needed to pitch the balance of the styling just right. This is a car with a story to tell."

To ensure the Exalt achieved his goals, Vidal pitched 10 exterior design teams against each other to meet his brief, and four interior teams also did battle. Internal competitions to lead design projects are not unusual in car companies – but to pitch quite so many people head to head is.

"The Onyx supercar concept was our guiding force," says Vidal. "That set the design philosophy, and especially the principle of having an emotional relationship with a car that sets it apart, led by the use of materials. At this end of the market, you are not buying the car because you have to. You are buying it because you want to. The Exalt is very distinguishable as a modern Peugeot – look down the side and there are just three lines, as is our DNA – but we also sought to pick up on details that would make the design unique. We have the heritage to build this sort of car with total authenticity. The echoes of the 504 coupé are no accident. We've shown that we can do simple lines with depth and animation successfully before."

From its panel-beaten body, evoking the spirit of 1920s car making, through to the so-called shark skin material that adorns the rear end, cleverly improving its aerodynamic efficiency to allow it to cut through the air, the Exalt wilfully blends contrasts with the goal of redefining luxury for the modern age.

Classic, elegant, piano key-inspired switchgear offsets a digital control panel that rises from the centre console, for instance. Simple, elegant fabrics, carefully created to avoid all but the smallest amount of visible stitching, sit alongside ornate, hand-crafted (and in places knotted and cracked) wood that fills much of the interior, peaking with the striking carved lion and bamboo piece that's set into the front passenger door, where it is most visible to the driver.

And note how driver-orientated this car is. China's luxury car market has long been dominated by sales to buyers obsessed with rear legroom but, says Gazeau, that is finally changing. "Today, China is about conspicuous wealth and travelling in the rear of the car, but we are challenging that," she says. "We wanted a car that would inspire its owner to drive and enjoy it, that offered touch points that were ultra high-tech, but others that were a link to their homeland and history, that would stir their soul."

Vidal is in no doubt that the Onyx and Exalt form part of a journey for Peugeot. After all, a mass-market brand can't hope to redefine the luxury car sector overnight. But a foothold in China and a changing landscape among post-recession buyers elsewhere might just provide the opportunity that Peugeot needs, both to break free of established conventions and to boost its battered profit lines. And if it can achieve that, who's to argue that the automotive landscape won't be richer for it?

ROMAIN SAQUET, EXTERIOR DESIGNER "The design must create an emotional relationship between the owner and the car. The cut into the body side at the rear conveys lightness and agility, for instance. The rear haunches are strong, but not all about muscle. They convey a sense of purpose, like an endurance racer."

SG "The so-called shark skin on the rear is a fabric with a micro-dot texture that helps airflow. Think of a golf ball with its dimples; this is the same. It has been tried in the aeronautical industry to save fuel, and we estimate it could save 2g/km of CO_2 on a car like this. And, of course, as well as a function, it has a stylistic role."

RS "Our solution for the rear glass looks complex from afar but, actually, it is one of the most production-ready aspects of the car. The double-bubble solution for rear headroom has been proven on the RCZ. The front window solution is more for the concept; meeting regulations with this style would be very hard."

PIERRE-PAUL MATTEI, PROJECT DESIGN DIRECTOR "Pure Blue is an air depollution filter system that maintains air quality while you are driving. It stops thin particles like nitrogen dioxide and sulphur dioxide from entering the car. In polluted cities – such as some of those in China – these are important considerations."

P-PM "Pure Touch is a new innovation, but we think it can reach production. When the car is empty and locked, it sprays a product on all surfaces to kill all bacteria and fungi. Think about all the touch points in a car and how dirty they get. And think about it, too, in the context of a polluted city."

ALESSANDRO RIGA, LEAD DESIGNER, INTERIOR "The cockpit is designed around the driver. You have our signature small steering wheel, and a dash that angles to the driver. The touchscreen emerges from the dash and is also configurable. It is like the screen found on the 308, but with many advancements."

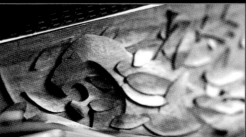

SG "The wood is black ebony, which is found in Asia. It is a very malleable wood and very striking in colour. We asked three Chinese sculpture experts what Peugeot stood for and chose this design as it combined our lion with Chinese bamboo leaves. The key is that it is locally sourced; that adds a premium quality."

GV "The stretched, piano-style toggle switches are an evolution of the toggles found today in the 3008. We want the most common interactions with the car to be more refined and a less technological – and more luxurious – experience. They are totally configurable, so the controls become individual to the driver."

2014's best features

Over the past 12 months we've been treated to some fascinating new cars. First impressions count for a lot, but there's nothing quite like putting new metal to the test against its closest rivals to find out how it really measures up. Over the next few pages we pitch some of the year's most important new cars against a wide pool of foes in a series of comparison tests designed to find out if the newcomers could become class-toppers.

We also paid tribute to a departing rally-bred icon from the east, celebrated 25 years of the Land Rover Discovery and rejoiced in the UK's current car-making boom. A vintage year indeed.

GRAND MASTER
FLASH

The new Mercedes C-class brings luxury and grandeur
to the compact executive market, but is it enough to
outshine its rival from BMW? **Matt Saunders** decides

PHOTOGRAPHY STUART PRICE

The C-class takes its cues from the luxurious S-class

Car making is, by nature, a competitive business, particularly at the top of the food chain. If Mercedes-Benz wasn't right now introducing a brand new C-class saloon on to the global market, parent company Daimler's balance sheet would soon record the consequences. Daimler itself would concede that the current benchmark for the new car is set by the BMW 3-series – our compact executive saloon champion and the car against which the Merc's various accomplishments are about to be measured. And so the exercise we're about to engage in makes perfect sense. And yet something doesn't feel right.

Your author's understanding of classical music is quite rudimentary.

But, inspired by the incredible Burmester sound system in this latest C-class, it's good enough to know that this new Mercedes is no more a direct response to the BMW than Handel's Messiah was to Bach's Brandenburg Concertos. The new 'C' sets out to achieve something entirely different than the BMW 'Three'. I'd bet there has never been a bigger ideological space or notional point of difference between the two cars than that which exists now that the W205 Mercedes-Benz has been launched.

Just as the 3-series managed two years ago, the new C-class succeeds its predecessor spectacularly well, setting new class standards in almost all of the ways Stuttgart intended. Inevitably, the targets Munich aimed for several years earlier aren't quite

as well covered. Does the latter make the Benz any less accomplished or alluring? Not a bit of it, and certainly not to C-class clientele. Which isn't going to make picking a winner today an entirely straightforward task.

The comparison with those two classical composers, by the way, isn't entirely spurious. Bach and Handel were born in the same year, it transpires, in towns just 50 miles apart in central Germany. Becoming the leading lights in a grand new musical art form, the two might have developed a rivalry fierce enough to poison their creative talents for perpetuity. Thankfully, they didn't. Recognising that they served different missions, masters and visions, they evidently understood that the classical canon had room

enough for both of them and ended up great admirers of each other's work. Amazing what Google can teach a distracted pleb, isn't it?

Sounds like the kind of relationship that BMW and Mercedes are nurturing these days. Because, as it turns out, a new Mercedes C220 Bluetec sits entirely comfortably on the asphalt next to a BMW 320d, just like those two mighty compositions might on a concert bill. While this Mercedes cannot do everything, its act has been sharpened and its shortcomings addressed. Its character, meanwhile, is even more discrete and inimitable than ever. The last thing it is, as we'll go on to explain, is an alternative to a BMW 3-series. And thank God that it isn't.

So the real question is this: which

In pure performance terms, the two cars are evenly matched

The BMW makes 181bhp and 280lb ft from its 1995cc

C-class delivers 168bhp and 295lb ft from its 2143cc

Both rode on 18s; run-flats for the 320d

BMW looks assertive, Merc graceful

is the more convincing in 2014? Swabian luxury done small-scale and more lavishly than ever before, or leaner and not so lavish 'modern premium' perfection cooked up by those notorious Mercedes 'admirers' down the road in the Bavarian capital? Place your bets, meine Damen und Herren.

SMALL-SCALE GRANDNESS

Observation number one: there's suddenly a lot of S-class about the new Mercedes C-class. The outward resemblance is striking enough that, following at a couple of hundred yards' range on the motorway and without a convenient neighbouring reference point with which to judge relative scale, you can easily mistake one for the other.

That the C-class can pull off that kind of visual impression tells us a lot about the direction in which Mercedes has taken the car. Company men speak of the desire to put genuine luxury and top-drawer refinement back on the compact executive menu.

So there's a great deal of old-school European grandness about this new compact Mercedes. Its gentle curves and classic proportions are all elegance and grace. They could hardly contrast more starkly with the assertive visual strength of the BMW. Chances are you'll respond to the styling of either the Mercedes or the BMW, but not both. For what it's worth, I'd suggest you're more likely to notice the BMW; you'd probably say the Mercedes is prettier. But that's just a hunch.

With a superstructure now made from just under 50 per cent aluminium, the C-class has trimmed down by 100kg compared with the outgoing steel version, and it has class-leading aerodynamic efficiency to deliver newly competitive fuel efficiency and CO_2 emissions figures. Like its bigger Benz siblings in more ways than one, it's now available with optional Airmatic air suspension – a first for the compact executive segment and a feature of our test car in particular.

The mid-spec Sport-trim C220 Bluetec automatic – Mercedes' forecast big-volume derivative and the car you see here – enters the market just one tax band higher than BMW's equivalent 320d EfficientDynamics and three bands →

SIMPLE TACTILE LUXURY AND MATERIAL RICHNESS
IS BATTLING MODERN BUSINESS-CLASS COOL HERE

← lower than the 320d Sport xDrive auto that BMW supplied for our comparison. Taking the BMW's four-wheel drive system out of the equation and strictly comparing like with like, a 320d is still 45kg lighter than a new C220, and because it has the edge over the Mercedes on power output, the BMW also wins a power-to-weight ratio advantage. But the Mercedes' torque-to-weight ratio beats that of the BMW, making the on-paper performance difference between the two cars only very slight; a manual C220 hits 62mph from rest two-tenths of a second more slowly than a manual 320d. Note to self: if the cars end up feeling that closely matched on the road, one of the BMW's main selling points will have been seriously eroded.

Air springs give the Merc a refined ride

3-series gives outstanding engagement

The BMW is marginally the cheaper of the two at entry-level price, but by hundreds, not thousands. Mercedes insists its car is better value when adjusted for standard equipment, and by more than a few hundred pounds, as it happens. It's also likely to enter the market with better residual values than the older BMW. So the cars will, in all likelihood, be evenly matched for both company car drivers paying contract hire and for private buyers.

A CABIN TO SAVOUR

So far, so little to go on. The picture becomes clearer, though, when you begin to compare things such as cabin ambience, passenger space and interior quality, at which point – by and large – the Mercedes-Benz new boy builds an early lead.

The BMW is marginally the more spacious car in which to travel, its driving position lower and more recumbent, its rear quarters marginally the more generous on headroom. But the Mercedes has, by a distance and in spite of all that, much the more pleasant and distinguished cockpit.

Simple tactile luxury and material richness is battling modern business-class cool here – and the former wins hands down. The quality of the mouldings, leathers and trims that make up the C-class's interior is both redoubtable and effortlessly superior to what you'll find in the 3-series. The Mercedes' seats feel softer, thicker and more cosseting. Its fascia fittings are much richer and more substantial, from the dashboard plastics →

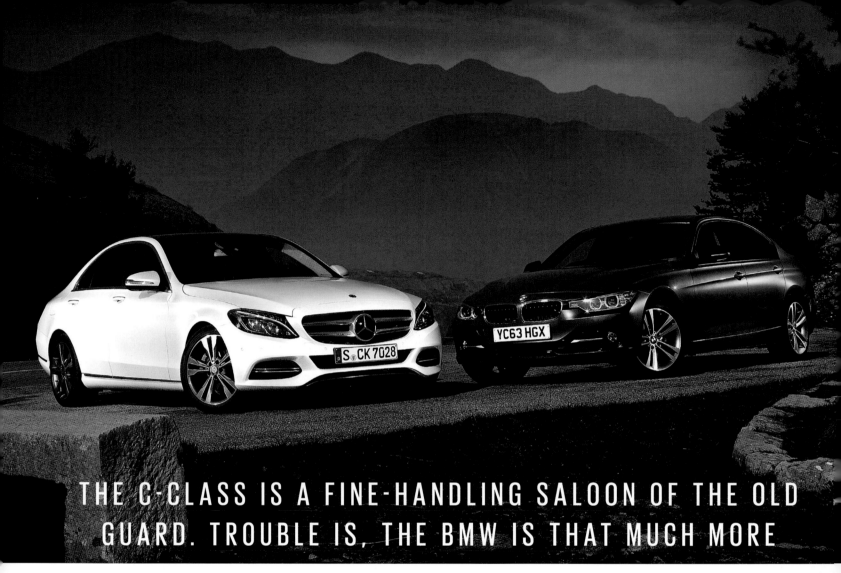

THE C-CLASS IS A FINE-HANDLING SALOON OF THE OLD GUARD. TROUBLE IS, THE BMW IS THAT MUCH MORE

← outwards. Everything about the C-class looks and feels expensive and laboured over, in fact. In the BMW, while the overall impression is plush enough, here there are material high points and low notes.

If the 320d's four-cylinder turbodiesel is slightly clattery and boisterous at idle, the previous C-class's was a bigger offender still. By comparison, the new Mercedes is smoothness personified. Considerably quieter than the BMW on tickover and low on vibration, the Mercedes is also remarkably well insulated from wind and road noise. On refinement alone, it feels a cut above the BMW – more than a match for a Lexus IS300h, even, which is really saying something.

The engine is big on low-end torque but lacks flexibility and high-revving punch. It's at its best serving up generous pulling power hovering at 2500rpm and under about 70 per cent throttle, as the torque converter shuffles through the gear ratios with elastic, unhurried ease. You can drive the C-class surprisingly quickly like this, with little sense of the speed you're carrying because everything is so effortless and so seamless.

But you can't drive it as quickly as a 320d. Above a certain point – when you're in manual mode on the seven-speed transmission, picking your gearchanges and keeping the accelerator buried for extended periods – the C-class begins to run out of reserves. The extra noise that the engine begins to make when stretched like this just isn't worth the very marginal gain on your rate of acceleration as you probe that last inch and a half of pedal travel. You can't hustle a C220 Bluetec along.

The very opposite is true of the 320d – perhaps partly because the car is slightly noisier at laid-back speeds. Even so, the BMW diesel's operational range seems twice as wide as that of the Mercedes. From 1500rpm to 4500rpm, the 3-series is ready to respond whenever and however you like. It also goes harder than the Mercedes under full power, while paddle-shift gearchanges from its eight-speed automatic transmission come more smartly, too. Even when you're not pushing the car along quickly, that makes the 320d relaxing and assured to drive in a completely different way to the C220.

On top of that, the 320d proves to be the more fuel-efficient car of our German pair in real-world use; 46mpg on our mixed test route answered 42mpg from the C220 Bluetec – and the former with a four-wheel drive system to take the edge off its return, don't forget.

The car that won a five-star road test verdict from us two years ago is beginning to show its hand. And it isn't finished yet.

A DYNAMIC MASTERCLASS

You can guess how this bit goes. As well we know, Munich's 3-series sets an exceptional dynamic standard on any given road, mixing civility with sporting poise like little else. It was untouchable in that regard before the new C-class came along and it still is now. And, since we might as well be upfront about this, offering that extra bit of agility and verve to interested drivers still makes the 320d our outstanding executive saloon. So the 320d wins.

But that's in no small part because keen drivers like you and me can't help but be seduced by BMW's vision of the modern sporting exec, as well as the current 320d's particular execution. And if, instead, you prefer a vision of a traditional luxury four-door kept quite small but still done by the book – with all the refinements, accomplishments and trappings that modern car making can provide – buy a C-class. It's that simple. The Merc isn't a poorer executive saloon so much as just a different, more traditional take on the concept.

The C-class is, in fact, stronger in the core disciplines where a generic luxury four-door should be strong. Its air springs suspend a body that wafts over a gradually changing road surface more imperviously than the BMW's on its steel coils. There's also better wheel control and a quieter secondary ride about the C-class than there has been about air-sprung Benzes of the past decade. We can't speak of the Mercedes' standard steel chassis set-up yet, but the only major trade-off of the Airmatic suspension is the lack of connectedness you sense with the road surface. But are you sure you want to feel connected to the road when Mercedes can insulate you from it with such suave effectiveness?

It may not be spry, but the C-class is gentile and easy to use. It may not be involving, but it's consistent and precise in its every move. It

has better cornering balance and sweeter steering than something so dedicated to comfort really deserves. The C-class, then, is a fine-handling executive saloon of the old guard.

Trouble is, the BMW is that much more – more game, more alert, more rewarding and more broad-batted. The 3-series offers three-quarters as much dynamic talent as the C-class in its guise as an unobtrusive everyday cruiser, but twice as much as a sporting prospect.

For us, so much has long been true. But, now more than ever, our main protagonists aren't adversaries as much as they are perfect contrasts to one another. More importantly for some, what these cars say about their owners is clearer now than it ever was. The BMW says: "I'm going places. I'm ambitious, exciting. I'm the next big thing."

The C-class has less to prove. While its statement is made more quietly, it replies with: "I'm established, successful, the definitive article. You go your way, I'll go mine."

To me, one of those positions seems vastly more self-assured and attractive – but it doesn't belong to the winner of our test. The BMW 320d is still very much the Messiah and will take some unsticking yet. But in the new C-class it has found a worthy contemporary at last. △

Material choices and quality of finish mark out the C-class's cosseting cabin

BMW's cabin has a more functional feel than that of the C-class, but still impresses

	1 BMW 320d Sport xDrive automatic	**2** Mercedes-Benz C220 Bluetec Sport auto
VERDICT	★★★★★	★★★★⯪
Price	£32,825	£32,860
0-62mph	7.4sec	8.1sec
Top speed	142mph	145mph
Power	181bhp at 4000rpm	168bhp at 3000-4200rpm
Torque	280lb ft at 1750-2750rpm	295lb ft at 1400-2800rpm
Gearbox	8-spd automatic	7-spd automatic

ULTRA VAUX

Aussie-built Vauxhall V8s are fun but crude, right? Wrong, says **Richard Bremner**. On the right road, the new VXR8 is more than a match for a BMW M5 or Mercedes E6.

PHOTOGRAPHY STUART PRICE

R11 VXR

t's about three miles long, this road, as it crosses open, sandy heathland. And it undulates. Nothing severe, but there are fairly gentle crests and dips – the sort that will fit just inside the wheelbase of one of these cars – and a bit of camber variation, too, the road's nearside edge occasionally sinking. By the standards of Britain's roads, it's not too bad, and there are no potholes. So why describe it? Because this is a road to prise open cracks in the armour of these cars – one of them especially so. But what armour these cars have. If you crave horsepower – lashings of it, with a king-sized side

order of torque – then these three are your kind of car. And ours.

The reason for this 1721bhp clash comes from Down Under. Holden Special Vehicles' GTS is the Aussie brand's latest high-performance machine, based on the latest VF Holden Commodore saloon. Which is a whole lot more modern than the previous iteration, coming with Insignia-derived infotainment and driver aids ranging from blindspot monitoring to a head-up display. So while it might look as traditional as a Vegemite sandwich, it's rather more sophisticated. When imported here, the HSV GTS mostly becomes a

Vauxhall VXR8 GTS – mostly, because it's not hard to find an HSV logo, most obviously on the steering wheel boss.

This is a substantially different beast from the previous VXR8, to the tune of an extra 148bhp and another 140lb ft. Its hulking 577bhp 6.2-litre Chevrolet Camaro V8 has a supercharger strapped to it and will stoke you a 546lb ft slug of torque at 3750rpm. Never mind the peaky appearance of this torque figure; it's enough to vault the VXR8 past 62mph in 4.9sec. You'll be putting in a bit more (admittedly enjoyable) work than in the other pair to achieve this, the VXR8 GTS being fitted as it

is with a six-speed manual gearbox.

The Vauxhall weighs a little less than the portly 1945kg BMW M5, at 1882kg, if not the 1870kg Mercedes-Benz E63 AMG S, but a more substantial difference is to be found in its price list: the Vauxhall costs £54,499. Not only is this tens of thousands less than its two rivals, but it is also only £5000 or so more than the previous model, which had substantially less power and kit. Much of that improved value is down to a more favourable exchange rate.

The E63 AMG S makes for a startling contrast, at £84,110, and the Competition Package edition of the

← M5 costs barely any less, at £80,205. That 'Competition' element provides an extra 15bhp, in case the standard 552bhp isn't enough. Torque? The full fat 502lb ft gush starts at 1500rpm and doesn't abate until the crank strikes 5750rpm. The M5 may be overweight, but that's still enough to slam it through to 62mph in 4.2sec. The powerhouse that does this is a fabulous twin-turbo 4.4-litre V8, which is mated to a seven-speed dual-clutch automatic transmission with paddle shifters.

These mechanical arrangements are pretty similar to those found in the Merc. It, too, is the version for those who feel the standard E63 isn't enough, this S edition mustering a vital extra 28bhp to bring the total to 577bhp. Which just happens to be the same as the Vauxhall's output. You probably won't feel the S's difference on the road (your wallet will, though), but against the watch it shaves 0.1sec off the explosion to 62mph, bringing it to 4.1sec. The power source here is also a V8, this one of 5.5 litres, its twin turbos spooling up 590lb ft at 1750rpm and keeping the flame stoked all the way to 5000rpm. The transmission is a seven-speed auto equipped with paddle-shifters.

So which car's armour cracked on that heathland road? Amazingly, the BMW's. It's amazing because we rate the M5 highly, even if it's a bit short on soul. But on this road, those undulations have this car heaving four-square on its wheels, sometimes to the point of discomfort, and its slightly darting nose needs a correcting hand over camber changes. It borders on being a minor handful. And that's in the softest of the BMW's three suspension settings.

The Benz is a calmer place to be. It's firm, even in its dampers' most pliant setting, but you won't be badly jostled or feel the need to back off because its body control is fading. Mind you, both suspension and some interior fittings clatter over rougher asphalt.

Experience the Vauxhall on this road and you enter an unexpected world of dynamic refinement. Its chassis is pliant and absorbent where the BMW's isn't, allowing you to proceed in calm at unabated pace amid your growing surprise. Tweak the so-called Driver Preference Dial to graduate from Tour to Sport and the magnetic dampers firm a little, as does the electric power steering, while the exhaust takes on a deeper, more resonant timbre. But you won't feel a lot more jostle, and the same applies even if you turn the dial through Performance to Track. It's no Mercedes-Benz S-class, but you won't be uncomfortable, either.

The M5 is far from disappointing in other departments, however, and among its more impressive talents is the business of changing direction. Turn the wheel and it noses into corners with the kind of measured eagerness that brings mid-engined configurations to mind, the liquid precision of its movement a real pleasure. This is a car with great dynamic balance. Raise the pace and it's hard not to marvel at the impressive exercise in mass containment that it represents, as nearly two tonnes of metal thunder through a succession of switchbacking sweepers.

VXR8's cabin lacks the quality feel of its German rivals, but doesn't want for kit

An offset steering column detracts a little from the E63's mostly appealing cabin

Well appointed BMW's interior gives the greatest sense of quality and class here

The VXR8 takes more commitment to make its tail break away, but all three are deliciously easy to control in a drift

The Vauxhall's steering you feel through a faint electronic fog. It's responsive, you soon realise, and actually quite precise, but your hands will always palm at its substantial wheel as if through woollen gloves. None of which seriously impedes your willingness to charge hard in this car, especially as it turns out to have decisively more grip than the BMW, which is all the more surprising when you consider that it runs narrower rear tyres. Proof of this came during our test track cornering shots, the VXR8 requiring noticeably more speed and commitment to make its rear end break away. Standard-fit torque vectoring must get some of the credit here. Getting the M5's rear end to slide is much easier, active diff or not, although both are deliciously easy to control once they're drifting.

The same applies to the limited-slip diff-equipped Merc, which hangs on for longer than the BMW but not quite as long as the Vauxhall. But the Benz has cleaner steering than the Australian car and turns with slightly more eagerness, although it can't match the BMW for turn-in. It corners flat and quite often feels like a track car, despite having a relatively supple ride. Which starts to disappear if you swivel the small rotary centre console knob between Comfort, Sport and Sport Plus. That's quite a lot of choice, and there's more besides, what with the three-position dampers.

Performance? Pile-drivers, all three of them. Never mind that the VXR8's peak torque arrives well after the Table Mountain curves of the other pair kick in; the Vauxhall's supercharger delivers a rippingly →

The big difference here is the VXR8's rather Australian, no-nonsense nature

← strong surge of thrust from little over 1000rpm and just keeps on going, the whining backing track adding to the excitement. It's the Mercedes that provides the best accompaniment, its V8 issuing a threateningly malevolent growl whose intent hardens in Sport. It's the quickest-accelerating car here. The Merc's seven-speed auto slurs perfectly, the exhaust's shifting pitch goading you into holding the throttle flat to 155mph. Although you won't be doing that unless you're on a track.

There's slightly more of a crescendo to the BMW's power delivery, and it's none the worse for that. This car is super-quick, and if you configure it that way, so are the gearchanges of its dual-clutch transmission, their timing adjustable via a rocker by the gearlever. The lack of a 'P' for park position is pointlessly baffling, incidentally, this over-complicated

gear selector requiring that you leave the car in Drive to lock the transmission and, indeed, the car. And while we're banging on about ergonomics, the Merc's steering wheel is almost astonishingly askew, its column spearing decisively towards the car's centre line. For this driver, though, the AMG's seats cause more discomfort, being noticeably less cosseting than those in the others.

If you want the aura of luxury with your performance, the BMW is the winner here. Its finely trimmed cabin oozes quality and class, if not quite as much of it as you'd expect in a car costing over £80,000. The same applies to the Mercedes, only less so. Its dashboard finish is of a slightly lower calibre, the uncharacteristic rattles from its trim often breaching an otherwise civilised peace.

The Vauxhall falls somewhat short in this department, as might

be expected, given its £25k price difference and its mainstream origins. Sure enough, the doors issue a mild but unbecoming clang when they're slammed, there's quite a lot of unyielding plastic inside and the seat leather looks as though it came from particularly ill-nourished cows. But it's certainly not all bad. You get decent-looking slivers of carbonfibre, plenty of brightwork, double-stitched Alcantara, a good infotainment system and much else as standard, besides the amusement of performing a Vauxhall versus HSV logo count.

From the outside, the VXR8 is decidedly less subtle than the others, but you can order a subtler rear wing. And it's actually the Merc that wins the grille mesh acreage contest. But you're not going to win prizes for taste if you choose this Vauxhall. Instead, it's the subtlety of its road manners that scores it so many points.

Later in the day, we find some quiet stretches of road that include tight, open, traction-testing bends, some unusually long straights and more of the crests, dips and camber shifts that test suspension systems so hard. On those straights, it's the premium pair that manage the most manically exciting launch towards the next county, even if the Vauxhall is hardly slow. The Mercedes feels secure and well planted, if at times a little agitated, while the BMW is again bothered by sine waves of undulation. The Vauxhall is barely troubled at all by such surfaces, besides being as aurally refined as the German duo at high speeds. And all three play ball on that tight, open corner if you dial the traction control down.

But the big difference between these three is the VXR8's rather Australian, no-nonsense nature. You can play with its switches if you like, but from the off this is a surprisingly easy car to drive, a car that encourages you to drive it hard and one that doesn't bite back when you do. There's no escaping the fact that this feeling is heightened by its manual transmission, whose gearchange is cleanly co-operative, if short of that final polish, but it's the fundamentally entertaining character of this car that will win you over. In the German cars, you must cut through a layer or two to get at their not inconsiderable best; the Vauxhall is game, while the other two are merely deeply able. And the BMW only on less rippled roads.

The source of the M5's disappointment has to be the Competition Package, this £6700 option perversely reducing the car's competitiveness by over-stiffening its chassis with 20-inch wheels and sports suspension. And the extra power is neither here nor there. Without these unnecessaries, the M5 would be a far keener contender. The S version of this E63 AMG Benz, on the other hand, is unspoiled by the upgrade, the (not inconsiderable) £9995 that you pay for the extra 28bhp and 59lb ft also providing a limited-slip differential and some styling enhancements.

But the result is that, for sheer driver engagement, the Vauxhall shades these two. What's even more surprising is that it rams home this advantage with its superior body control on testing surfaces. Add in the extra grip, more comfortable ride and the fact that it offers much the same standard of telematics as the German pair for an all-in price that's £25k lower and its victory looks startlingly clear. True, there will be plenty reckoning that you need to grow up if you drive home in one of these, and its value in three years' time might be cause for sober reflection, although neither the E63 nor the M5 is a star performer here. The premium pair are a whole lot better on the emissions and economy fronts, however.

Vauxhall can bring no more than a 100 VXR8s in under the low-volume Japanese Type Approval import arrangement that makes this car possible. And it reckons on selling no more than 30 or so, as it did last time around. Drive this version, though, and you'll conclude that it deserves a wider audience than that. And if you're a Holden sentimentalist, consider that this Commodore will be the last built in Australia, with GM closing the factory in 2017. On a brighter note, Holden will continue, as will HSV, and Vauxhall plans to continue importing its cars. If they match this standard, that's something to feel good about. Ⓐ

In a straight line, the VXR8 is the slowest of the three, but it's still a very rapid car

The German cars are closely matched for acceleration, but the Merc is a tad quicker

	1 Vauxhall VXR8 GTS	**2** Mercedes-Benz E63 AMG S	**3** BMW M5 Competition Package
VERDICT	★★★★½	★★★★☆	★★★½☆
Price	£54,499	£84,110	£80,205
0-62mph	4.9sec	4.1sec	4.2sec
Top speed	155mph (limited)	155mph (limited)	155mph (limited)
Power	577bhp at 6150rpm	577bhp at 5500rpm	567bhp at 6000-7000rpm
Torque	546lb ft at 3850rpm	590lb ft at 1750-5000rpm	502lb ft at 1500-5750rpm
Gearbox	6-spd manual	7-spd automatic	7-spd dual-clutch auto

EVO &OUT

Mitsubishi's Evo has reached the end of the line. **Matt Prior** goes for a final fling in the best of them all

PHOTOGRAPHY STAN PAPIOR

On one website dedicated to the Mitsubishi Lancer Evolution is a page summarising the model's development.

They're all there: from the original Evo I of 1992, through the II to the III that took Tommi Mäkinen to the first of his four consecutive world rally championships. It passes the IV, V and the 1999 Evo VI, to this: the limited-edition Evolution VI Tommi Mäkinen Edition of 2000.

Then the page stops. There is more, of course, but forget the rest, it suggests. The decade that took in evolutions seven through to 10? Forget it. Forget all from the Mäkinen onwards. After the Mäkinen, it suggests, there is nothing.

Harsh? Maybe, but this is, even today, considered the Evo's pinnacle. The best the breed ever offered.

Ostensibly, the Mäkinen Edition, sometimes known as the Evo 6.5, was built to celebrate the Finn's fourth world title. Under it was an Evo VI, but with a new titanium turbo and a different exhaust, a reworked front bumper with fewer lights and more scoops, 17-inch Enkei alloy wheels, a Tarmac-style set-up on the suspension and a quick steering rack. Power was 276bhp, like most top Japanese performance cars of the day, and torque 274lb ft. A good, square, balanced power and torque output.

These were still, just, Group A rally car days, and although newer World Rally Championship regulations were putting greater distance between road and competition cars, Mitsubishi was persevering with existing regulations, which maintained a link that meant the Mäkinen Edition was something special.

It still is today. This car is one of just 250 officially sold in the UK. The full livery and red paint weren't compulsory, but I wouldn't have it any other way. This one is low on miles but we've been encouraged to enjoy it as we please, which means that we've got to drive it. There's little to be enjoyed in the basic interior, after all. And looking at the outside only makes you want to fire it up. So we do.

Why now? Because this year Mitsubishi UK is importing just 40 examples of the Evo X – specifically in FQ 440-MR specification – but that'll surely be it for the Evo as we know it. There should be another Evolution, but it won't be quite like this. We're saying cheerio via the best there is.

We choose Stoke-on-Trent for the pictures, because we want urban and moody. There are areas of decay and regeneration here, but there's no analogy to be made. Comparing a place to a car always understates a city's past and patronises its present and future. But some of the old brickworks look right, and it's close to the Peak District for a thrash.

RALLI ART

Y851 GHW

Life after Evo

Where next for the Evo? That's not what we intended to talk about with Mitsubishi's global product director, Gayu Eusegi, at the 2011 Geneva motor show, but he told us anyway. "There is still a demand for the Evo, but we must stop," he said. "Our influence is now EV technology."

It was unequivocal talk that sent Mitsubishi's European PR into meltdown, suggesting we'd misunderstood or that Eusegi had been mis-translated.

But now, as an Evo X comes back for one final hurrah, things for the Evo — at least, as we know it — look bleak. We hope and expect that there will be another Evo-badged car, and with electric motors controlling where and how the power is sent — like the company's Pikes Peak racer (above) — it could be spectacular. The body will be different, and the drive will be different, but here's hoping some of the original Evo magic remains.

On such roads, the car's size and agility are welcome assets

The 2.0-litre four-pot turbo makes 276bhp and 274lb ft in its standard guise

The driver's view is unremarkable, but the rewards intense

The trip there is a reminder that, although I still think of the Evo as a modern car, and 2000 is not very long ago, things in motordom change quickly. The Evo feels small – at 4350mm long and 1875mm across the mirrors, it is – and you are perched higher than I remember inside, with a low window line; visibility is terrific.

Those seats sit high but are good, mind. They're extremely supportive, and although the steering wheel adjusts for rake only, you can find a position that's comfortable over distance. What's more wearing is the tyre roar, which drowns any engine drone made by a powertrain that encompasses that highly charged 2.0-litre engine and a five-speed manual gearbox. Both respond with

reliable precision. There's a little turbo lag, but it's far more compliant and responsive than many a turbocharged modern engine. I don't want to sound like a Luddite – more modern cars are exceptional – but by gum, this is a lovely thing.

I'm sure I remember the ride being considered harsh, but today, although it's firm and mid-corner lumps kick back through the quick steering (about 2.1, maybe 2.2 turns), there's not the harshness that I expected. There's no crashing. The tyres, 225/45 R17s, are relatively modest. Gosh. I really like this car.

By and by, we're through with Stoke and heading out on to the open road, and I like it more and more. How can you not? It weighs just 1365kg, for

heaven's sake, and has a body that's tied down better than a Ford Fiesta ST's yet rides easily and comfortably. It steers better – with linearity, accuracy and feel – than any of today's power-assisted set-ups.

And you're able to approach its limits on the road, to feel its extraordinary agility. It seems to pivot around its middle, although not in a nervy, unstable way. It changes direction on a whim. The permanent four-wheel drive system uses active yaw control, meant to limit understeer and oversteer, but on the road in somebody else's classic car (how curious it feels to write that phrase about an Evo, but I suppose it is), I'm not inclined to delve too deep. But even at seven, eight – oh, okay, if

you insist I'll have nine-tenths – it is truly, seriously terrific.

It's still great value, too. A Mäkinen Edition – price new, £31,000 – can't stay at the £10k-£15k mark that it demands now, surely. It's just too good for that. This isn't just the best of a breed we're saying farewell to here. It's the best of any breed. △

MITSUBISHI EVO VI TOMMI MAKINEN	
Price then	£31,000
Price now	£10,000-£15,000
0-62mph	4.4sec
Top speed	150mph
Power	276bhp at 6500rpm
Torque	274lb ft at 3000rpm
Gearbox	5-spd manual

FOR THE 4C-ABLE

The Alfa Romeo 4C touches down in the UK, and **Matt Prior** lines up a Lotus and a Porsche to welcome it

PHOTOGRAPHY STAN PAPIOR

IT'S CLEAR THAT THE 4C IS LOUDER THAN THE ASTON V12 VANTAGE S. A LOT LOUDER

Yikes, this is loud. For logistical reasons, I get into the Alfa Romeo 4C only minutes after climbing out of an Aston Martin V12 Vantage S, a car not particularly noted for its quietude.

Yet after a turn of the key and a brief roll through Slough Trading Estate (all motoring locations should be so glamorous), it's clear that the

4C is louder than the Aston. A lot louder. And boomier, especially on the motorway I head to next, owing, I suspect, to the optional sports exhaust fitted to this 4C and its ultra-stiff carbonfibre tub, which is the car's calling card.

It means the 4C – the most radical Alfa in decades – is built by Maserati in Modena, not alongside the Giulietta or Mito. I call it the most

radical for decades because, unlike the limited-run 8C, the new 4C isn't a cut-down Maserati with limited input from Alfa Romeo.

This is all Alfa. It has an all-new carbonfibre composite chassis, a new turbocharged 1742cc four-pot with an aluminium block to shave kilos off the ostensibly similar unit found in the Giulietta and, even though the 4C is built at Maserati's factory, it's to be

constructed in the thousands, not the mere hundreds. It's a significant car for Alfa, whose range now includes fewer models than Ferrari's.

That's why, now that it has arrived in the UK, the 4C warrants a full group test against what we perceive to be its closest (and undoubtedly greatest) rivals, which are waiting for it in the Peak District. We'll take the trio on the roads here, and then

The Alfa has a squared-off wheel and digital display

High-quality fit and finish characterise the Cayman's cabin

head over to Lincolnshire's Blyton Park driving centre for a little bit of on-limit handling testing.

Given its circa £45,000 price (although this one is £54,970 with options) and the fact that it has two seats and a roof, perhaps the obvious rival to the 4C is a Porsche Cayman, which arrives near this haven of caverns and reservoirs in slightly incongruous specification.

We know in our hearts that an S model with a manual gearbox and a limited-slip differential is the Cayman to have, but that mechanical set-up pulls itself too far from the 4C, whose 237bhp turbocharged engine with dual-clutch automatic gearbox is the only available powertrain.

To match, then, we've found a base 2.7-litre Cayman with the optional PDK dual-clutch auto transmission,

and although it has come on 19-inch wheels, its suspension and other options are left largely unaffected. Thus equipped, the Porsche costs a whisker over £50,000.

Meanwhile, failing to be dimmed even by the Peak District's drizzle, we've at short notice sourced (thanks to dealer Bell & Colvill) an orange Lotus Elise S Club Racer. Having driven the 4C in Italy, we took a bit of

a punt on wanting the Lotus involved and, as we'll see, even though it looks under-equipped on both cost and power in this company (packing just 217bhp and priced at £36,000), it proves to be a more pertinent choice than we could have imagined.

That's due in no small part to the fact that – as soon becomes clear – the 4C and the Cayman are not natural bedfellows. In fact, this much was →

Elise's steering shows up that of the 4C, but gearshift is sloppy

ON KNOBBLY B-ROADS IN THE 4C, THERE IS MUCH TO ENJOY

← obvious to the pair of us who drove them 200 miles to the location of this group test.

The Cayman, accepted wisdom told us, would be the more complete car, but the margin by which it is more cosseting is quite extraordinary. Even on its 19-inch wheels, it feels positively soft. Not in isolation, perhaps, because there is notable exhaust and road roar, but next to the 4C it feels like a Mercedes-Benz S-class, soothing away motorway miles thanks to its rock-steady steering (a hallmark of German manufacturers), its large seats and

a commendable audio system in its plushly finished cabin.

The Alfa's cockpit is pleasingly finished in places, too. The strictly digital instrument binnacle is natty and the leather/aluminium door pulls are sweet, although mixed in with it are heater controls that wouldn't lift a Fiat Panda's ambience, flat seats, poor rear visibility and a stereo that has more functionality than you might

initially think but which can't – even at its maximum setting – drown out the extraordinary boom from the engine should you breach 70mph. In the general cacophony, I don't know how much of the 4C's engine noises are exhaust, induction, tappets, cams or injectors – although I can tell you that a lot of it is turbo whoosh – or how much of it gets through because of the lack of soundproofing.

Alfa says it uses thin glass to keep weight down and claims that the 4C has a dry weight of 895kg (I'd reckon on adding 200kg to that when we put it on our scales) but, all around, materials are specified for stiffness and lightness (the front wishbones are bolted to the monocoque, not a subframe) rather than refinement. And it shows.

And the noise itself? It depends. It's certainly one that gets noticed. If you're feeling uncharitable, you could suggest that people's heads are turning to see which clapped-out Nova with a cherry bomb pipe is

cruising down their high street.

Listen carefully, mind, and you'll pick up the nuances of a highly tuned engine whose note owes more to a Lancia 037 than a Ford Escort RS Turbo. Eardrums thus attuned, following a 4C down the road is one of motoring's great pleasures, as you watch its seductive shape and listen to its engine rise and fall. I cannot think of a more evocative car launched in the past decade.

That fact puts you in mind to enjoy the Alfa. It's easy to want to like it, because (and although we don't usually dwell on aesthetics, I'm inclined to make an exception here) I think that it is quite the most extraordinarily good-looking car. Okay, it's quite short and the headlights aren't for everyone, but with this shape, and making this noise, I defy anyone with an ounce of octane in their veins not to feel predisposed towards it. Schoolboys stare and point in comedic fashion as if an Apache helicopter had just landed outside the Co-op.

Scooching around knobbly B-roads in the 4C, there is much to enjoy, too. Away from a motorway, you are freed, at least temporarily, from the ceaseless cabin boom, and the unassisted steering that felt nervy gains more intuitiveness and feel.

The 4C rides acceptably – firm,

but not too uncomfortable – yet feels agile, too. As speeds rise and corners come, you can sense the lack of inertia that comes from having a low kerb weight and an engine in its middle, and that the front is lightly loaded and a touch less reassuring as a result, than the Porsche's. Power delivery is overtly boosty, but on the road this is no big deal.

This is where the Porsche shines too, though. It steers sweetly (assisted, yes, and electrically, too); there's less feel than in the Alfa, but it's an accurate and intuitive system. The naturally aspirated engine is leggy, and because power builds slowly but inexorably towards the 7400rpm peak rather than boosting in quickly, and because the kerb weight is 1340kg, the Cayman feels less urgent and slower than the 4C. The magic in the chassis is all there, though. That a car so comfortable on a motorway can shine with such agility and feedback on a B-road is truly remarkable.

Inevitably, the Lotus feels more one-dimensional than the Porsche. Our tester fell out of it at the motorway services after a lengthy journey, imagining it to be the most wearing of the three (although he hadn't yet tried the 4C), but in the Peak District it is in its absolute element. It shows the Alfa how →

4C's boot capacity is a slender 110 litres

The Cayman swallows a full 425 litres

The Lotus's boot is similar to the 4C's

← oily, precise and millimetre-accurate an unassisted steering system can be, and although the Elise's manual gearshift is as ordinary as we've come to expect, the supercharged four-cylinder engine's delivery is wonderfully linear, too.

The Alfa's heady boost still leaves the Lotus feeling second best in the power stakes, but the Club Racer element of the Elise S adds an exhaust rasp to the 1.8-litre Toyota unit's sound, overwhelming the supercharger's whine. As a result, after the boosty but extremely fast 4C, the Lotus feels like a modestly quick naturally aspirated car, although little the worse for it. In our dash east before an overnight stop near Blyton, the Lotus is a joy. Less

so when it rains and the road and wind noise roars, but given the 4C's rawness, the Elise doesn't give so much away in terms of refinement.

We like Blyton Park, and the next morning it is dry. Our photographers would prefer that it had more elevation, but it is an enjoyable handling circuit in modestly powered road cars. The ideal place,

you'd think, for these three.

Here, though, the Porsche's specification plays against it. It feels less wieldy than the other pair, and as well it might, given that it is. It is softer and slacker of body control. Still, understeer is limited and the Cayman will very easily spill into tidy and controllable oversteer if you lift off upon turn-in.

The Porsche shows delightful poise and fluidity over challenging B-roads

The Alfa is rewarding but lacks the precision of its two rivals here

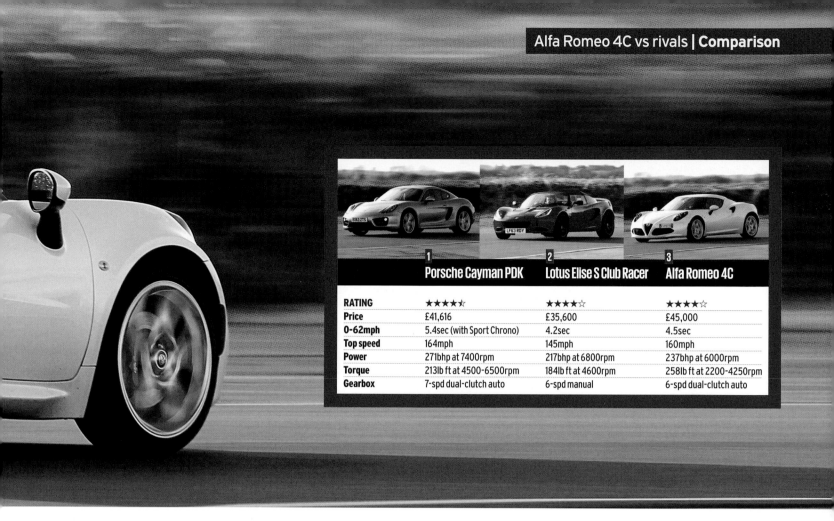

	Porsche Cayman PDK	Lotus Elise S Club Racer	Alfa Romeo 4C
	1	**2**	**3**
RATING	★★★★☆	★★★★☆	★★★★☆
Price	£41,616	£35,600	£45,000
0-62mph	5.4sec (with Sport Chrono)	4.2sec	4.5sec
Top speed	164mph	145mph	160mph
Power	271bhp at 7400rpm	217bhp at 6800rpm	237bhp at 6000rpm
Torque	213lb ft at 4500-6500rpm	184lb ft at 4600rpm	258lb ft at 2200-4250rpm
Gearbox	7-spd dual-clutch auto	6-spd manual	6-spd dual-clutch auto

It lacks precision, though, where the Lotus does not. The Lotus feels made for conditions like this, with its incisive steering, an initial onset of steady understeer that can be neutralised with a gentle lift, and throttle response that can trim its line easily thereafter.

And although the Alfa ought to feel made for these conditions too, it does not – not quite. The basic components of a world-beating machine are in here, beneath the admirable carbonfibre chassis and the heady engine. Like the Elise, the 4C has initial push away from the apex at the front, which can be tamed with a lift or a trailed brake, but the boosty engine's slowness of response makes neutralising the understeer, or entering into a generous slide, more difficult. At seven or eight-tenths, the little Alfa is pleasingly engaging and agile, but there's little of the chassis magic that separates a good car from a truly great one.

Does it matter? Arguably not. When the 4C goes, looks and sounds like it does, being a few polishes short of gleaming is not the greatest sin.

However, the inevitable conclusion is that the Lotus is superior to drive and no less tiring over a distance, while the Porsche is victorious because it remains the most complete sports car on sale. Best to think of the Alfa as different rather than last, though. Sometimes – and here, I think, it's unique in this company – simply nothing else would do. ▲

OCEANS APART

Chevrolet says its latest Corvette is more sophisticated than its predecessor, but can it really match its suave European rivals? **Nic Cackett** finds out

For a car with a 60-year history, well over a million sales and almost universal name recognition, Chevrolet has done a spectacular job of making the Corvette's occasional entry on to the UK market inconspicuous. Seen from the correct side of the Atlantic, the veteran nameplate has been an ownership sideshow, beloved by some for its rip-roaring, redneck eccentricity but too often pre-judged by others as a crude, gas-swilling rip-off.

In truth, here in the UK, the Corvette never seems to enjoy the heartfelt backing of its manufacturer. Initially, with the incentive of proper right-hand drive hastily promised, it seemed as though the C7 – righteous reclaimer of the Stingray name and product of six years' development – could be different. Then GM reneged on its offer of right-hand drive and now, with the Corvette inching back towards the beachhead, it's hard to see how much success can be expected, abandoned in the corner →

of selected Vauxhall dealerships as it is seemingly destined to be.

Conceivably, none of this would have mattered had the C7 been permitted to come ashore with a price figured by an online currency converter rather than GM's marketing department. In the US, the basic Corvette starts at just over £31,000. Here, in higher spec but with the steering wheel still attached to the wrong side of the dash, it starts at just over £61,000. However, with an all-new 6.2-litre V8 producing 460bhp, a seven-speed manual gearbox, detachable hard-top roof and a serious sub-4.0sec sprint in the offing, Chevrolet can argue that, even

by doubling the initial outlay, the car represents good value for money.

Chevrolet's insistence on higher profit margins means, of course, that we get to show the C7 – represented here in early non-UK spec and on winter tyres – no mercy in cherry-picking its rivals. Two of the European hosts awaiting the Stingray in the Brecon Beacons come with V8s: the venerable but still vital all-wheel-drive Audi R8 in its latest seven-speed S-tronic format and the cheek-puckering Jaguar F-type in 5.0-litre coastal barrage form.

The third rival may have only a bashed-flat 3.8-litre, six-cylinder engine with 395bhp, but it is also

THE C7 LOOKS AS INCONGRUOUS AS AN F-22 RAPTOR JET ON A WEDDING CAKE

our Top Trump among big-league sports cars. I drove the Porsche 911 Carrera S across to Wales, and three hours in its company only served to highlight just how difficult it will be for the C7 to land a glove on this quality of opponent. The 991 is a masterly exercise in meeting driver expectation; I own thermal base layers that feel less well fitted to the forearms and back than the Porsche's apparently organic control weights and hewn-but-homely interior. On the motorway, in horrendous conditions, its capacity for conveying sure-footedness is extraordinary; it takes an imprudent pedal stamp in virtually knee-deep rainwater for its

305-section Pirelli P Zeroes to slip worryingly sideways. Otherwise, it simmers on the softest setting of its (optional) adjustable dampers and barely challenges its PDK dual-clutch automatic gearbox as it lawn-stripes the sodden lanes of the M4.

The Corvette arrives last, looking as incongruous in Brecon as an F-22 Raptor fighter jet on a wedding cake. Its size partly counts against it, but not nearly as much as the mishmash of angles and bulges at work in the composite moulding. Its rear, brusquely styled with a set square, is a Confederate flag away from parody. Craven attention to aerodynamic enhancement is said to have →

Corvette lacks the tactile quality of its rivals' cabins

Porsche mixes its classy finish with an unerring driver focus

F-type's stylish cockpit masks the V8's rabid intent

R8's familiar cabin lacks the latest touchscreen tech

← dictated the C7's design, but compared to European slipperiness, its gullies, crevices, scoops and swathes are too obviously the by-product of deliberate styling pizzazz, not airflow.

Still, if it looks like a work of fiction, it sounds like savage mechanical fact. With the Corvette's small-block V8 turning, the engine's unchecked vibrations threaten to unscrew the cabin fascia. In a Captiva, that would be a problem; in the C7 it feels as though it's using the magnesium-framed seats to massage a 'no replacement for displacement' mantra into your nether regions. It's a fitting introduction to what's to come from the LT1 lump, even if it is slightly at odds with the Corvette's LCD overload elsewhere. An 8in touchscreen, digital instrument cluster and head-up display make good on Chevrolet's promise of jet fighter influence, and it's all ready to turn graphical cartwheels via the Drive Mode Selector dial, pre-loaded with five self-explanatory settings: Weather, Eco, Tour, Sport and Track.

Despite the addition of numerous optional interior packs, the C7 doesn't satisfy the fingertips in such a convincing fashion as the others. The 911 is more classy, the F-type is better looking and even the Audi, despite its age and lack of a touchscreen, is a more functional proposition. Trim and switchgear inferiority speak to the difference in price more obviously than elsewhere and, if you're sniffy about such things, clearly differentiate the Corvette from the luxurious ambience readily achieved in its European counterparts. But there are good omens: the steering wheel is now smaller, the throw from the stubby gear lever is pleasingly short and the reinforced grab bar on the console was apparently added after designer ride-alongs at GM's proving ground in Michigan.

The latter is a feature shared with the F-type, the only car here that comes as standard with an even more lavish output. Officially we don't like the 488bhp V8 S as much as the V6 S, although for some time I couldn't think why. The front end is more put upon, but at a fast cruise the flagship feels pleasingly substantial, with heavier steering and sterner damping countering the V6's slight flightiness. Like the C7, and more so than the 911 or R8, the experience is defined by the engine. A proper pantomime villain, it lurks three millimetres deep in the accelerator travel, dispatching Welsh B-roads in a ZF shuffle of fourth and fifth, tugging a contented chassis along in its wake.

I didn't even bother with the paddles until photographer Papior found a tricky stretch of wet road. Driven more aggressively for the camera, the Cain is suddenly readily apparent in the F-type's Abel. There's practically no understeer to speak of, just an immediate, transparent swish of rear-wheel slip – even with the traction control engaged. It's the same in the V6 S, but in the V8, appropriately enough, the natural flamboyance feels supercharged. While poise and Jaguar's quick steering keep it halfway approachable, the immediacy of 460lb ft from 2500rpm introduces premonitions of ditch-bound excursions into the proceedings.

Those thoughts linger in the C7. The new V8 develops 50lb ft more low-end torque than before and now exceeds the power-to-weight ratio of the 911. That's worrying, when the last Corvette I drove was the previous convertible Grand Sport, a car coupled to its wheels in much the same way as a priest is connected to the Almighty. Mercifully, the Stingray exorcises such questions of faith almost immediately. There's an electric motor aiding the power →

Porsche's 395bhp plays second fiddle to the Jag's 488bhp

THE CORVETTE MASSAGES A 'NO
REPLACEMENT FOR DISPLACEMENT'
MANTRA INTO YOUR NETHER REGIONS

steering now, and also a new variable-ratio rack, although the real advance has been achieved by making the system a whopping five times stiffer than before. The result is a verifiable relationship with the far-flung nose – numbed, yes, but still accurate enough to relay your intentions to the road.

It gets better. Once your line through a corner has been established, the C7 is capable of following it without the leaden reactions of a body not properly connected to its underside. That's because the rigidity so patently absent from the C6 has been in part fixed. The previously simplistic aluminium frame – think of a ladder and you're there – found beneath its unstressed composite body

THANKS TO ITS ELECTRONIC DIFF, THE STINGRAY EASES INTO SLIDES WITH LESS ABANDON THAN THE JAGUAR F-TYPE

panels is replaced with a far more sophisticated design that is 45kg lighter and assembled with a new GM-patented spot welding process.

True, its new-found dynamic cohesion is not in the same league as that of the R8 or 911, both of which bristle with sophistication through the same set of bends. The Audi, courtesy of its spaceframe, covers ground in unbelievable fashion. The Stingray's new-found stiffness has allowed the settings of its transverse springs to be kept agreeably supple, but the ride quality and negligible pitch and lean still look primitive next to the R8's unflinching ability to intimately hug the ground as it works out the best way to screw 424bhp into it. The 991 is even more agreeable; obedient and biddable through a

richer steering rack and superior dual-clutch 'box, it'll either nail itself to your conviction or, if you're purposefully hard on the sublime brakes and quick on the power, bust through its mammoth traction with the precision of a safecracker.

Compared to either, the C7 remains a dynamic lollygagger at the limit, although not an unlikeable one. Its rear transaxle layout leaves it with what Chevrolet says is 50 per cent front, 50 per cent rear weight distribution, and because the wheelbase is longer and both tracks wider than before, there's a bigger footprint to seat it on. Thus the directional stability, even on Michelin Pilot Alpins, is admirable. And thanks to an electronically controlled slippy diff – standard

	1	**2**	**3**	**4**
	Porsche 911 Carrera S PDK	**Audi R8 4.2 FSI S-tronic**	**Jaguar F-type V8 S**	**Chevrolet Corvette Stingray (C7)**
RATING	★★★★½	★★★★☆	★★★★☆	★★★★☆
Price	£85,835	£96,610	£79,985	£61,495
0-62mph	4.3sec	4.3sec	4.3sec	4.2sec
Top speed	187mph	187mph	186mph	181mph
Power	395bhp at 7400rpm	424bhp at 7900rpm	488bhp at 6500rpm	460bhp at 6000rpm
Torque	324lb ft at 5600rpm	317lb ft at 4500-6000rpm	460lb ft at 2500-5500rpm	465lb ft at 4600rpm
Gearbox	7-spd dual-clutch automatic	7-spd dual-clutch automatic	8-spd automatic	7-spd manual

for the UK as part of the Z51 performance pack – the Stingray eases into slides with less abandon than the F-type.

In this, it is ably abetted by the Corvette's finest feature. Ten million hours of computational analysis may not have eradicated the pushrods or squeezed more than two valves into each cylinder, but by persisting with the small block it has kept its unique temperament at the heart of the car's identity. So while the platform is clearly now more than just a trolley jack for the V8, the inherently slow-to-stir valvetrain works in the chassis' favour, demanding huge throttle openings before it'll let things get inordinately silly at the back then providing more than enough power to keep it that way.

And that's just in the corners. Keep the wheel halfway straight and the Corvette really romps along. Aided by an endless seventh ratio meant for meaningful fuel economy (26.7mpg combined is claimed), its top speed is registered at 181mph. Of possibly more relevance is the gulping forcefulness of its acceleration, which builds with the air-breathing V8's revs like the earth's temperature rises with its proximity to the sun. On the motorway home, out of the burly manual gearbox's third or fourth ratios, the head-up display was as much a counter for my incredulity as it was a recorder of actual speed. At full, inexorable chat, neither 7400rpm of Porsche flat six nor 7900rpm of Audi V8 is a performance peer of the C7.

Perhaps the journey didn't pass as richly as it did at the wheel of the 911, but with the adjustable magnetorheological dampers – another standard feature of European C7s – set to Tour, the Stingray plots a persuasive line between a mid-Atlantic plod and a genuinely European glide. Ultimately, it's in that slim stretch of sand, between the outgoing C6 and the assembled horde, where the Stingray successfully buries its past reputation. Objectively, it isn't a deadly serious match for the R8 or 911, even if it is £35k cheaper than one and £24k less than the other and capable of shaming both away from the lights. The Jaguar F-type, a good £18k more expensive itself, is more of a kindred spirit.

The Stingray is cut from a different cloth, certainly. It's bigger, lazier and trashier, but is also just as quick to press-gang you into a belly laugh or make you comfortable in its company. It makes the hairs stand on end, too, chiefly those aroused by a soulful V8 soundtrack and molten rubber rather than the goose bumps of fast progress. On balance, I'd spend more money on acquiring one of the others – most likely, given its all-round ability and quality, the 911 – but I can see why Chevrolet thought it could now send the Corvette anywhere in the world and be justly proud of it. And I'm glad it's still coming to the UK, even if the circumstances make its arrival that bit sadder and less relevant than it might otherwise have been.

NEW POWER GENERATION

The BMW M235i joins a set of affordable fast cars built to do things differently. **Matt Saunders** finds out if true greatness lies within it

PHOTOGRAPHY STUART PRICE

The most heinous crime that BMW's M division has committed these past 10 years, it seems to me, has nothing to do with turbochargers, flappy-paddle gearboxes or 500bhp SUVs. It's much more important than all of that. Despite trying a couple of times, how and why has Munich failed to create a worthy successor to the wonderful E46 M3?

To give them their due, both the E92 M3 coupé and the E82 1-series M Coupé were fine cars. They just narrowly missed that elusive mark. The E92 V8 M3 was, after all, £50k by the time it bowed out. The new M4 is going to cost a full £60k by the time you've added the bare-minimum options – hardly the stuff of irresistible performance value. And although the 1M was a very likeable, spunky little attempt at redressing the balance, it was also a car with a chip on its shoulder. The Grant Mitchell of M division history: pugnacious, →

Handling like this is good enough to give the BMW a clear advantage over the A45 and S3

← punchy, proper 'ard. It had 'handle with kid gloves' written all over it.

Let's say you were advertising for this new M car as though you were recruiting to fill a job vacancy. The classified ad might read as follows: "Wanted: dynamic, enthusiastic executive to enliven neglected area of business. Must be an excellent communicator with boundless energy, clear focus and sparkling character. Flexibility and pragmatism key. Must also be willing to work weekends. Sub-£40k starting offer; generous entertaining budget."

Three out of the four cars arranged on the page before you can be considered applicants for that 'situation vacant'. All three occupy the space in the performance market abandoned when BMW M elected to move its hot 3-series upmarket midway through the previous decade. Each brings something novel and interesting to the table. Eighteen months ago there was no such thing as a mega-hatch by Mercedes-AMG or a cheaper, leaner, better-looking little brother for the insipid Audi S4 in the shape of the new four-door S3. Meanwhile, we're still getting used to the idea of any BMW 2-series coupé, let alone one with 322 horsepower.

So could the new M235i be the perfect successor to our much-missed E46 M3 – or should we look for that heir in a less obvious place? And, should we find it, is that heir likely to survive a run-in with the best similar-priced two-seat sports car that the market has to offer right now: the Porsche Cayman?

In its pomp, up against a Porsche Boxster S of the same vintage, I reckon that an E46 M3 could have held its end up. Let's see what the new boys are really made of.

The obvious place to start is with the little differences that, perversely, have brought these three together. Mercedes-Benz A45 AMG, Audi S3 saloon, BMW M235i: see them afresh side by side, forgetting everything that we've written about the Mercedes these past 12 months and simply surveying what's in front of you, and here's what you'd guess. That the Audi is the priciest option, because it looks expensive – like a million dollars, in fact. That the Mercedes must be the poorer cousin on grunt and sheer speed, because it's a hatchback. And that the BMW can't be half as practical as either, because it's a two-door coupé. You'd be wrong on all three counts. Welcome to the topsy-turvy new age of German premium-brand performance choice.

The A-class tops the rankings on peak power and torque output, power-to-weight ratio and on-paper accelerative guts. It also has carbonfibre-trimmed door mirrors, a yobby (but optional) roof spoiler, standard four-wheel drive, a standard dual-clutch automatic gearbox and

Low-set Cayman's equally sunken driving position is pure sports car

The BMW's cabin lacks drama and errs to the ordinary

The S3 saloon's nicely judged interior has the best ambience by far

The A45's tacky red trim highlights won't suit all tastes

There's no point in a 322bhp rear-driver if you can't do this

an exhaust that pops loudly enough on full-throttle upshifts to disturb roosting birds several counties away.

It's 'only' a hatchback, yes, but it's as hot a hatchback as AMG can currently conceive of – and AMG can conceive of some pretty sensational things. And they hope that it's a vision you'll be willing to pay for, by the way. A good 10 per cent more for, in fact, than the competition it's facing today. Call me old-fashioned, but I'm not sure I like those terms.

Substitute its six-speed dual-clutch auto gearbox for a six-speed manual and the Audi S3 would occupy the opposite position: the cheapest option in the running. It's hard to believe, because you can't help reading a sense of superiority from the car's elegant three-box silhouette. German performance saloons cost a bit, don't they? Particularly those with eye-catching technical styling details inside and outside like this one. Well, no, apparently they don't – not

relatively speaking, anyway.

Still, a stretched S3 saloon must have more cabin space than a regular five-door hatchback, right? Er, no. The S3 saloon has precisely the same wheelbase as a five-door Sportback, as well as a more curvaceous roofline that's great at taking your headroom away. Jump from one back seat to the next in these cars and you'll soon realise that the A45 actually offers the most rear cabin space.

Smaller adults and growing kids

will be comfortable in the back of all three cars, but large adults won't be comfortable for very long in the back of any of them. There lies one of the bigger compromises for those with 'only' 30-something-thousand to spend on their German sporting option in 2014.

Adults will find getting in and out easiest in the Audi but, once they're in, they'll be surprised to find little more headroom and legroom than they will in the BMW – the two-door. Really. →

The A45 is the quickest – and not just off the line, but at any speed

← Boot space in the BMW and Audi is identical. Both offer more below the parcel shelf than the A-class does.

In short, there's little to separate the three on usability. The versatile nature of a hatchback body means that we'll give the A-class the nod. But giving credit to the most practical car in a group like this is a bit like giving a prize for 'best dressed' at the local YMCA. The BMW does a smidge more than you expect from it, the Audi a bit less. But all three do only just about enough to be reasonable choices as everyday transport.

A seductive, powerful, mechanically rich powertrain is a must in a car like this; it's what the Germans have always done best. 'Efficient' has stolen in among those touchstones over the years but, while it matters to a point, it's something

of an impostor in a description of any machine within this particular little niche. And anyway, even in 2014, how many buyers in this market genuinely wouldn't be willing to indulge a bit of a thirst for unleaded in a car that made it truly worth indulging?

You'd instinctively describe only one of our trio as worthy of that kind of indulgence – the one that covers all of those bases with consummate ease. And it's neither of the four-pots.

The Mercedes A45 AMG's 2.0-litre turbo, mated to its four-wheel-drive, dual-clutch automatic transmission, is bludgeoningly effective but peaky and a little contrived. The S3's slightly lower-strung turbo has more natural charm and a more obliging manner about it but less outright fierceness. But the BMW's engine is something else entirely: silken, superbly flexible

and utterly melodious in full voice.

The Mercedes is quickest – and not just off the line, but at any speed, as soon as the turbo has spooled up. Away and rolling, its advantage over the Audi is large, and marginal but undeniable over the BMW.

You feel the need to flatten the accelerator fairly frequently, though, just to get value out of the AMG. Off boost, the engine is a bit flat and toneless, the gearbox a touch frustrating in manual mode. Oddly spaced gear ratios can make it tricky to judge which cog you need and increase the likelihood of asking for one that the gearbox then simply refuses to give you.

Soft throttle response, meanwhile, occasionally inhibits engagement with the grippy chassis on your way out of a bend. Traction feels mighty.

Cornering balance is a touch blunt to begin with, but it improves if you're aggressive with your inputs. Bottom line: you have to throw off the layer of stability covering the A45's dynamic talent like a waterlogged puffer jacket before it'll start to really entertain.

The Audi is just as stable but feels better balanced and more responsive in every way. You'd accept its deficit on full-power pace to the AMG in return for those things. It helps that the Audi's cabin is much the nicer, lighter place to be – leaving the retina-transplant two-tone sports seats to one side. It's roomier up front, too. It must also help that you get wider tracks in the S3 saloon than you do in either hatchback, as well as MagneRide adaptive dampers as standard-fit equipment.

It takes time to find the best driving

mode in the S3. The car's Individual mode allows you to dial up the engine and gearbox response but ratchet down the suspension and steering settings. Thus configured, there's consistency and user-friendliness to the wheel, which lets you merrily probe away at the edges of the car's handling potential, should you choose. There's a pleasingly sticky, precise front end here, and a rear that's gently mobile when it's unloaded and the ESC is deactivated. Which is about as much as you could hope for, really. Nice work, Audi.

You should hope for much more from the M235i – thanks, perhaps, to the memory of that old M3. Insert dramatic pause here, then. In terms of ultimate handling perfection, your hopes aren't answered quite as emphatically as they might have

been in this car. The top-of-the-range 2-series does have a great engine, but also slightly problematic steering and a lively, engaging sort of chassis that's merely very good.

Faint praise? Not a bit of it. Handling like this is good enough to give the car a clear advantage and selling point over the Audi and the Mercedes. Good enough to deliver its owner a more engaging and rewarding drive than he or she will get in almost any other compact coupé we can think of, actually. But not quite great; not quite the grand second coming. And nothing to compare with the Porsche that has been loitering in the wings all this time.

Old-fashioned communicative honesty is probably the biggest asset that the M235i has. The optional adaptive M Sport suspension has →

S3 saloon's cabin isn't as big as you'd hope

A45's interior is the roomiest

The M235i is more practical than it looks

Cayman is strictly a two-seater

you flicking between Sport and Comfort modes over most UK roads, but in both settings you know exactly how the car will respond to sudden steering inputs or a mid-corner bump. The Comfort setting is the better option most of the time; that's when the ride is at its most level and fluent but still feels taut and tied down.

And yet still the M235i hops, squats and squirms. It'll do it more slowly and gently if you want it to or, at higher speeds and effort levels, more suddenly and a bit more savagely if you firm the dampers up. The rear wheels chirrup and slip sideways slightly under full power as the car comes alive beneath you.

There is unchecked body movement to account for during fast direction changes. And there's no standard limited-slip differential – so the handling at the car's limits isn't as controllable as it should be. There's a good basic balance of grip here and several times as much scope for a bit of throttle steering as in the AMG or Audi. But there isn't quite the delicacy that you'd ideally want. What a shame.

It takes a truly great sports car like a Porsche Cayman to shine a spotlight on the M235i's deficiencies – to make you aware that greater poise and purity are on offer not too far north of M235i money, for those willing to accept the usability compromise.

The Cayman is barely quick enough in a straight line to keep up with the S3, let alone the Mercedes or the BMW. But that just doesn't matter. The Porsche's idiosyncratic flat six is perfectly governed by the right-hand pedal, and spinning it up to and beyond the 5000rpm mark is like taking a hit of amphetamines. Porsche's steering rack shows both the Audi and BMW how to execute a flawless, progressive system – quite conservatively, and with feel. The Cayman's body control is breathtaking and effortless. Its handling is exactly as flamboyant or as benign as you want it to be at any particular moment. This is a car to lose yourself in – one that melts away in front of you. On road or track, it has that rare

It takes a truly great sports car like a Porsche Cayman to shine a spotlight on the BMW M235i's deficiencies

All three are close rivals but each gives something different

	1 **Porsche Cayman**	**2** **BMW M235i**	**3** **Audi S3 saloon**	**4** **Mercedes A45 AMG**
VERDICT	The best drive here by a distance. Special.	Plenty of pace, handling richness and desirability.	Handsome and punchy with tidy handling.	Fast, but made to look pricey and a bit one-dimensional
RATING	★★★★☆	★★★★☆	★★★★☆	★★★★☆
Price	£39,694	£34,250	£34,720	£38,190
0-62mph	5.7sec	5.0sec	4.9sec	4.6sec
Top speed	165mph	155mph (limited)	155mph (limited)	155mph (limited)
Power	271bhp at 7400rpm	322bhp at 5800-6000rpm	296bhp at 5500-6200rpm	355bhp at 6000rpm
Torque	214lb ft at 4500-6500rpm	332lb ft at 1300-4500rpm	280lb ft at 1800-5500rpm	332lb ft at 2250-5000rpm
Gearbox	6-spd manual	6-spd manual	6-spd dual-clutch auto	7-spd dual-clutch auto

power to make the difference between the course, speed and attitude you intended to take and those you've actually taken negligible. So small, in fact, that you can kid yourself that it really isn't there at all.

But then a Cayman is built expressly for such things, with a great deal more freedom than any BMW. Could any front-engined BMW ever be that good? Perhaps not. But your author is sure of two things, when all is said and done. Firstly, that for something that's intrinsically so much more humble than the Porsche – complete with usable back seats and costing several thousand pounds less – the BMW M235i makes an excellent addition to our motoring world. And secondly, that Munich's account remains in debit to the tune of one brand new, 14-plate E46 M3. ◭

With the Porsche, you trade practicality for ability

On absolute speed, the A45 AMG takes no prisoners

The BMW has a compelling blend of all-round appeal

The S3 saloon represents a lot of car for the money

VOYAGE OF

DISCOVERY 2 (1998)

This one's a 1999 3.9-litre V8 prepared for the Camel Trophy. The Disco 2 had a longer rear overhang and was heavier than the first but was essentially the same, except the regular diesel option was a pokier five-pot. Tough, but spoiled in the rear by its seven-seat layout.

DISCOVERY 1 (1989)

The first Discovery, surprising for its superb long-travel suspension, low-rate ride, spacious and airy cabin, the beat of its tough 2.5-litre turbodiesel four and its vast range, courtesy of a 90-litre tank. With permanent four-wheel drive, it's still a very capable off-roader.

DISCOVERY

The Discovery is celebrating its 25th birthday. **Steve Cropley** looks back at four generations of Land Rover's million-selling off-roader

PHOTOGRAPHY STUART PRICE

DISCOVERY 3 (2004)

Complete change for the Discovery; the Mk3 was bigger and much more advanced than its predecessors. It still used a massive ladder chassis, but with all-independent suspension, electronics to seek out traction and a 2.7-litre V6 diesel engine that introduced unprecedented levels of refinement.

DISCOVERY 4 (2010)

Improved Disco 3 with its (more frugal) engine expanded to 3.0 litres and an eight-speed ZF auto to save even more fuel. Better electronics, too. 'Discovery' script across the bonnet of this recently facelifted version signals an intent to apply the name to a range of models.

For a snapshot of how the British motor industry has grown in the past quarter of a century, look no further than the range offered by Land Rover in 1989, just before the Discovery was launched. Back then, dealers had just two products to sell their customers: the farmer-friendly Land Rover Defender and the swanky Range Rover, the pair positioned so far apart as to be almost comical.

Things couldn't stay like that, and they didn't. The gap has been filled over the years until today it contains four models that last year shared most of Land Rover's sales of 425,000

units. But, truth be told, the whole move began with the launch of the Discovery, which has since sold just over a million copies.

Twenty-five years ago an air of expectation surrounded Land Rover as spy pictures gave fuzzy details of a mysterious new 'leisure' model codenamed Project Jay. Launching a third model seemed a bold step for a company still recovering from the upheaval of nationalisation (1975) and privatisation (1988), but in world terms Land Rover was actually years behind the game.

The Japanese, who understood world markets better than anyone,

had been expanding sales of their Shoguns, Patrols, Land Cruisers and Fourtraks. Partly because of these, and helped by a growing US vogue for lifestyle 4x4s such as the Ford Bronco and Chevy Blazer, a demand for softer off-roaders was growing in Europe. Between 1983 and 1988, sales of 4x4s expanded from 80,000 to 200,000. The figures look paltry now, but they disguised a four-fold increase in demand for leisure off-roaders, and by the mid-1980s even the preoccupied management of Land Rover had spotted the trend.

That word 'even' isn't intended to denigrate those in charge at the time.

It's just that within the nationalised environment, things took years longer than they should have. It had taken 10 years for the original Range Rover to be made as a four-door and 16 for it to be launched in the US.

There were other distractions, too. Even as the Discovery project was starting in 1986, hundreds of Land Rover stalwarts were protesting a plan espoused by Mrs Thatcher to sell Land Rover to GM. (They occupied Hyde Park as a protest and were so effective that Number 10 did a deal with British Aerospace instead.)

What we didn't know then was the extent to which the Discovery would

BY LAND ROVER'S GLACIAL STANDARDS, THE DISCOVERY WAS DONE IN RECORD TIME

Steve talks Discoverys with long-serving Land Rover man Roger Crathorne (centre)

change life at Land Rover. Against the glacial timetables of previous projects, it went with amazing speed. Led by Mike Donovan, the company decided a fast-to-market leisure model would need to use existing hardware and know-how, so it settled on Range Rover underpinnings.

From then on, the Discovery was created in record time, using procedures previously unseen at Solihull but still in use today. "The Discovery was our first entry into a project team environment," says John Bragg, head of engineering at the time. "It was far more efficient than anything we'd done before. One of our

bosses referred to us as the paperless society, because team members carried much detail in their heads. If someone had left at the time, we'd have been in all sorts of trouble."

Only now, looking back over the Discovery 1's nine-year life from a decent distance, is its essential 'rightness' visible. This is what we were doing one sunny morning last week at Eastnor Castle, near Ledbury, the magnificent country estate on which the off-road abilities of every Land Rover since 1970 have been developed. Irrepressible heritage expert Roger Crathorne, a 50-year company man, had brought one of →

IT STROLLS OVER EASTNOR'S BUMPS WITH A PLEASANT, LOW-RATE GAIT

← each of the four Discovery models and I was to be treated to a ramble through the model's history.

We started our exercise with a fine Discovery 1. Not just any example, either, but the first saleable unit: a highly prized 2.5 Tdi 200 diesel from the company's heritage collection that has done only a handful of miles and is in better-than-new condition.

I remember plenty about this model's launch, having been among the pressing crowds that watched its unveiling at the Birmingham

motor show in 1989. The company had also revealed it in Frankfurt a few weeks earlier – in a bold attempt to underscore its challenge to international rivals – but this was very definitely the main event. We might have been dismayed that the vehicle they unveiled was a two-door (or three-door, if you counted the single side-opening rear door), given the 10-year gestation of the four-door Range Rover. But Land Rover had already revealed that a four-door Discovery was less than a year away.

To inject some drama and shroud the pragmatic decision to use Range Rover running gear, bosses engaged product designer Jasper Conran to create a new interior, a move that really drove the public's imagination. Not all of Conran's innovations made production (he visualised, for example, a sunglasses holder in the steering wheel boss), but features such as the adventurous grey-blue upholstery and a holdall that zipped into the car's actual console made positive headlines.

The exterior designers also excelled. Although the dimensions, weight, chassis, coil suspension and steel inner body structure (beneath aluminium outer panels) were all close to the Range Rover, the Discovery had its own identity – a major achievement given that the pair shared the same scuttle and windscreen. But the Discovery's two-level roof, with revolutionary skylights, gave it a character that has driven its styling since.

On the outside, decals were the

Disco 1's relaxed, ambling ride suits the manner of its 2.5-litre turbodiesel engine

Discovery 1's roomy, Jasper Conran-designed interior broke new ground in 1989

Contemporary, kit-laden Discovery 4 shows how the SUV game has moved on

thing. Land Rover used them to imply modernity and make the difference between its new model and the more tasteful Range Rover, although they didn't last long. The customers just didn't like them.

Even after 25 years, it's the drive that impresses. Our early model's meaty 111bhp turbodiesel had a rattle about its idle that always seemed reassuring and remains so today. Plug the short gearlever into first and the memory of rifle-bolt shifts flood immediately back, along with the

sure stroke of a long-throw clutch. The Discovery strolls away from rest and over Eastnor's bumps with a gait that is ridiculously pleasant as long as you don't hurry, although these days suspension engineers would probably want to tame this generous set-up with more powerful damping.

There are more major surprises. One is a fuel tank capacity of nearly 90 litres, which allows even this somewhat old-tech diesel to do 600 miles between fills, something that always underscored the expeditionary readiness the Discovery's name implies. Another is the glassy, low-waisted character of the cabin and the exemplary space. The two-door Discovery 1 has short front doors that make access to its rear quite difficult by modern standards, but once passengers are installed they find the rear compartment's room and comfort impressive – more impressive, in fact, than the Discovery 2, which arrived in 1998 and had its middle row of seats squeezed forward to make space for a pair of forward-facing chairs at the very back.

We move on to the Discovery 2, a specially loaded version configured for Land Rover's former global torture test, the Camel Trophy, which continued until tobacco sponsorship moved beyond the pale. Roger →

Clockwise from top left: 2.5 Tdi (Mk1), 4.4 V8 (Mk3), 3.0 TDV6 (Mk4), 3.9 V8 (Mk2)

←Crathorne rides along, but he isn't struck on the 2, what with its cramped rear and an extended rear overhang that hampers serious off-roading.

Still, this is a beguiling edition: a five-door V8 auto, nose-heavy in comparison with the four-cylinder 2.5 Tdi but superbly torquey and smooth, with a sedate burble curling up to your ears. With a four-speed automatic, it's luxurious but sedate. And thirsty; this is the version, someone said, that made the Discovery's big tank a necessity.

Diesel and economy lovers could by now choose the 136bhp five-cylinder Td5 diesel 2.5, whose maximum torque of 221lb ft at under 2000rpm is its main event. This unusual engine is just as durable as the rest, says Crathorne, but depends more than earlier engines on electronics for correct functioning. This is inclined to deter those who use Discoveries to cross trackless wastes and expect to mend out-of-sorts engines with hammers and screwdrivers.

Forgive me if I don't dwell on driving the Discovery 3 and Discovery 4. This is not to imply a lack of love or respect; the reverse is true. It's just that these are modern vehicles about which we've written enormous tracts in recent years. Too many people have said too many times that Discoveries 3 and 4 are essential utility vehicles for any other conclusion to be contemplated.

These two introduced V6 diesels of increasing brilliance and frugality – first a 2.7 and then a 3.0 – and lots of electronics to find traction where the naked eye would swear there was none. However, the styling is the thing for me. The Discovery 3's lead designer was a bloke called Andy Wheel, and from the first day his work was revealed at the end of 2003, I've admired its gracious, neatly chiselled lines above those of any other SUV.

Which is why, to this day, assessing capability against cost, the Discovery 3 is my favourite of the four. Back in 2005 I ran a welly-green Autocar long-termer for 25,000 miles and had very serious designs on buying it. Our activities included a tough expedition in Iceland that it survived without acquiring so much as a nick in an alloy wheel. Naturally it had to be shipped back from Iceland, and I was looking forward to its arrival one morning – and to negotiating a buying price – when the phone rang and it was the man from Land Rover. "Your Discovery won't be back, I'm afraid," he said rather bluntly. "There was fog on the M1 last night. The transporter jack-knifed and your car fell off the top deck."

The pain took me by surprise. A member of the family had passed. The Missus, who loved that car, was upset for a week. Other Discos were offered, but it wasn't the same. For a long time I preferred to drive something else. Maybe a Discovery 4 would fix it. Might be fun to find out. Ⓐ

WHY BRITAIN'S CAR INDUSTRY IS BOOMING

How it's booming again, why it's booming again and what it has done to get here. **Hilton Holloway** explains

ast year the British car industry built 1,509,762 cars and 87,671 commercial vehicles – a total output of 1,597,433 units. It also produced 2,553,316 engines.

On current projections, made by the Society of Motor Manufacturers and Traders (SMMT), the automotive sector will build around two million vehicles in 2017, finally beating 1972's record.

The UK car industry is on a roll. And the recent recovery could be judged all the more remarkable considering that in 2009 – in the wake of the bursting of the global property bubble – the UK made just one million new vehicles. In just eight years, output will have doubled.

Our auto industry seems to have an ability to clamber out of what can look like terminal decline. In the comparatively short – but very sharp – recession of the early 1980s, the industry hit rock bottom, making 887,679 new vehicles in 1982. But in the second half of the 1980s, industry output sustained a near-continuous rise, peaking at 1,786,623 in 1999. It then fell, collapsing from 1,446,619 in 2008 to 999,460 in 2009.

At the current rate of rise – and helped by a European car market that has finally switched from contraction to expansion – the UK car industry is forecast to build 1.57m units in 2014 and 1.72m in 2015 and go on to reach 2.04m in 2017.

Truth is, Britain's automotive output today is relatively modest. Indeed, the UK is only the 14th biggest maker of cars globally. According to 2012 figures, we are behind France (1.68m) and Spain (1.53m) and hopelessly adrift of, say,

fifth-placed South Korea, which built 4.17m cars, and first-placed China, which built 15.52m cars.

Even so, our automotive industry is vitally important to the wider economy. According to the SMMT's 2012 calculations, the UK's car industry turned over £60bn – around three per cent of the UK's economy. Its £31bn of exports totalled around 10 per cent of all UK exports.

The UK's post-crash recovery has undoubtedly been aided by the fact that 77 per cent of the vehicles

Britain's annual car-making output is forecast to top two million units by 2017

Jaguar's output will
increase significantly
with the new XE saloon

38,500

Around 38,500 people are employed in UK motorsport, 25,000 of whom are engineers

UK car design has come of age

20 seconds

A new car rolls off a UK production line every 20 seconds

←made in the UK were exported. And half of that number went to countries in the European Union.

One vital area of the UK car industry that is still racing to catch up is the supply chain of component manufacturers. The UK is something of a powerhouse when it comes to engine manufacturing, and the SMMT says it is possible to build 80 per cent of a typical car with UK-made parts, but the nation's supply chain still needs to expand. The good news is that "18 out of the world's 20 biggest automotive suppliers" have a UK base and 82,000 people are employed in the supply chain, so the foundations are in place for healthy expansion.

That's where we are today. If we are to hit the SMMT's estimate of two million vehicles by the end of 2017, we will have to produce and sell an extra 100,000 vehicles each year for the next four years. So where are these new sales going to come from? And how will the boom continue?

Firstly, and most importantly,

we've got big investments coming from Jaguar Land Rover, a company that is making massive profits and investing big money in new models.

While production of the all-new Range Rover and its Range Rover Sport sister car is well under way, they will be joined by a new flagship Discovery model. There will also be three new medium SUV models, headed by the new Jaguar 4x4, which will be augmented by a smaller Discovery and a smaller Range Rover. Added together, we could expect as many as 250,000 extra SUV sales from JLR by 2018.

However, the biggest single model boost for UK plc will be Jaguar's new XE, an all-aluminium rival for the BMW 3-series. With an estate version also on the way, expect another 160,000 sales from Jaguar in three or four years' time. And that's not to mention JLR's huge new Wolverhampton-based engine facility, which is currently gearing up for production of the new four-pot 'Ingenium' engines.

We should also see a big boost for Mini over the next couple of years as the third-generation family comes on stream. Last year Mini's Oxford plant made around 175,000 cars, but it has capacity for more than 50,000 on top of that. And it's likely to fill that capacity, says BMW, because it expects the upcoming five-door Mini hatchback to sell very well.

The new 'sports estate' Clubman will also be more of a mainstream premium rival for cars such as the Audi A3 Sportback, rather than a quirky small car. Indeed, the expected shift of the Mk3 Mini into the mainstream car market also reveals the limitations of expansion in a single country when exports are so significant. BMW is so confident of the need for extra capacity for the new Mini that it will also build the model at the Dutch Nedcar factory that used to build Volvos and the Smart Forfour.

We will also see a substantial investment at Bentley (although output will be in the thousands, not the tens or hundreds of thousands) for the company's new SUV, a sister car to the forthcoming new Audi Q7. Bentley will also become the global manufacturing centre for the Volkswagen Group's W12 engine.

Another surprise investment has already begun at Nissan's remarkable Sunderland facility. The Japanese company wants to try to get a European foothold for its Infiniti premium brand, and to this end it is investing £250m to install the facilities to produce its new Mercedes A-class-based model.

So it seems that the UK automotive industry – barring another economic shock – is finally set to break the 1.92m-unit production record set in 1972. Which raises the question: just what has the British car industry done to get back into contention, albeit after four decades?

The reasons why vehicle production plunged by one million units – around 50 per cent – from 1971 to 1982 are pretty much the reasons why the British car industry nearly collapsed: fragmentation, big losses, poor production engineering, poor product planning, labour disputes, a weak supplier base, limp export performance and the arrival of superior imported cars.

In such a state, the British industry was also not prepared for the economic crunch brought on by the 1973 oil crisis and from the increased competition from European brands that came when the UK joined the Common Market.

According to Chris Cowin's book, British Leyland: Chronicle of a Car Crash, the 1960s were a period of heavy consolidation across the →

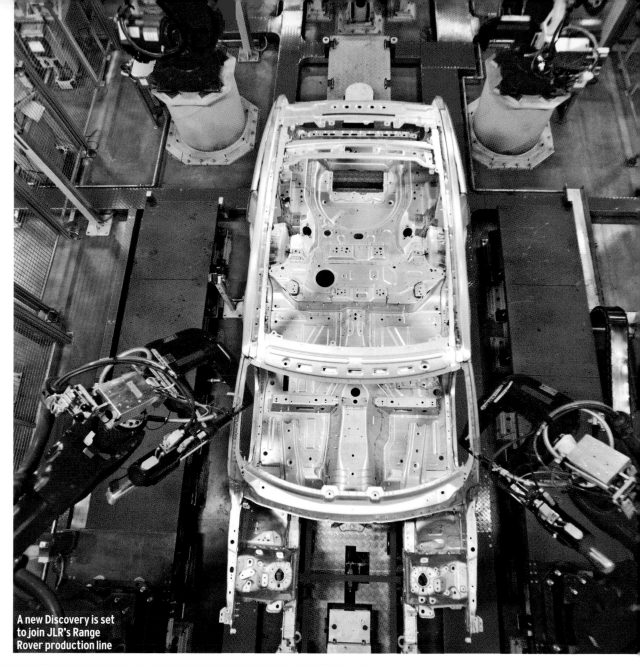

A new Discovery is set to join JLR's Range Rover production line

4200

UK car manufacturers make on average more than 4200 cars a day

← European car industry, and the British car industry was no different.

In 1966 Tony Benn of the day's Labour government tried to negotiate a three-way mega-merger between BMC, Leyland and the failing Rootes Group. In the end he managed to forge the British Leyland Motor Corporation merger, made up of 48 plants and 190,000 people in the UK and 66 plants abroad. Even in 1968, BLMC was Britain's biggest exporter and the world's fifth-largest car maker. But it all proved to be downhill from there on.

Perhaps the core reason why the UK-owned car industry collapsed was explained to me by Sir Michael Edwardes, who was the boss of BL from 1978 to 1983. He revealed that when he arrived, he drove an early prototype for what would become the Maestro. He thought it so poor that he began lobbying the government to allow him to seek out a technology partner for BL. "We had lost the ability to engineer a good car," he said.

By the 1970s Britain was desperately short of top-flight engineers. No bespoke technical and engineering schools had been built after World War 2 and the engineers who had trained during the war years were retiring. The few replacements went into aerospace, or at least steered clear of the car industry. Even the legendary Sir Alec Issigonis did not complete an engineering degree.

Sassy commercial decisions were also few and far between. Again, graduate management trainees were thin on the ground and roundly loathed by shop workers and bosses who had come up through the ranks.

The divisions in British society were not just class-based; the regional rivalries between the merged plants of the BL combine were just as bitter. The industrial strife is well documented, but perhaps not the internal conflict over 'differentials', which were the jealously guarded wage differences between the different trades inside a factory.

The sheer industrial paralysis of the 1970s is shown clearly in the 10 years it took Jaguar to launch the (unreliable) XJ40, the eight-year gestation period of the (unreliable and uncompetitive) Maestro and the six or so years it took to get the (outdated) Metro to market. The Metro, of course, was no more than a Mini with a hatchback body and an improved engine.

The long turnaround began in the early 1980s with BL's partnership with Honda, which showed that the BL workers could build a very reliable car when it was properly engineered. It was the investment of time, money and engineering skill that Ford

'JLR's expansion best exemplifies the results of 25 years of retraining'

endowed on Jaguar (and later Land Rover) that transformed the XJ40 into the best-selling X300. It was BMW's foresight and skilled planning that allowed the Range Rover and Mini brands to be rebuilt.

BMW's policy of letting Rover pursue its own ideas shows how important external management guidance was to the British industry. When the Rover 75 emerged from its BL-style five-year gestation period in 1999, it was the wrong car at the wrong time. As one manager put it to me recently, "We went retro just as everyone else went dynamic."

Evidence of the turnaround is also seen in Nissan's skill in exploiting British instinct for clever new concepts, and never more so than when the firm gave the green light to the Qashqai project. Expecting to sell around 80,000 units a year, the Qashqai has been a worldwide hit and is arguably the most successful British car of all time.

British styling also came of age at the end of the 1980s as a result of highly trained graduates emerging from Coventry University and the Royal College of Art (fresh designs like the Austin 1100 and Aston DB5 were Italian and the Mini and first Range Rover were both pure product design). We still have a shortage of engineers, but we now have a government that says it is committed to "the march of the makers".

The expansion at JLR best exemplifies the results of these 25 years of on-the-job retraining and reskilling. The company is now netting huge profits (probably the biggest ever seen by a British car maker) under its own steam and is enjoying the highest profit margins in the global industry.

With real strength in depth when it comes to engineering, quality, planning and styling, the British car industry is today in the best shape of its 120-year history. ⏹

Exporting wealth
The average value of our exported cars is over £20,000 — up 70 per cent from 2007

£12,000

£20,000

2007   2014

82,000
The UK automotive supply chain employs around 82,000 people

The Mk3 Mini will be built in Holland as well as Oxford

BRITAIN THE BRAND

The positives of Britishness in car design are old news to Ralf Speth, CEO of JLR, despite the fact that he was born in Bavaria and spent his first 20 years as an engineer working for BMW.

"In the town where I grew up, there was one E-type," he recalls. "It was unobtainable – a dream. The only Land Rovers were Defenders, and these were icons, too. They were never normal cars, which is why it is such an honour now to work for JLR."

Speth was one of the volunteers who, in 1994, answered BMW's call to help run Rover. He also worked here for Ford's PAG, then stayed to run Jaguar and Land Rover when they were bought by Tata in 2008, taking the helm as CEO in 2010. A large part of his job is to promote Britishness, which he sees as a unique asset.

"Britishness is tangible," he says, "but it is also hard to define. It stands for a very special lifestyle that often involves country living. It also stands for being liberal and tolerant. It plays well around the world, though there are occasional times when it doesn't

always go according to plan."

Speth remembers the time our PM had a meeting with Tibet's spiritual leader, the Dalai Lama, and thus torpedoed JLR's Chinese business for several months. But it recovered.

"Britishness is visible in our cars," Speth says. "When you see the shapes and read the lines, you can see they're different. Land Rover design chief Gerry McGovern refers to 'a killer combination' of British design and engineering, and he's right."
STEVE CROPLEY

Speth says Britishness is built into Jags